POWER AND ITS PARADOXES

A Convoco Edition

CORINNE MICHAELA FLICK (ED.)

Convoco! Editions

Convoco Foundation
Brienner Strasse 28
D – 80333 Munich
www.convoco.co.uk

British Library Cataloguing-in-Publication data: a catalogue
record for this book is available from the British Library.

Edited by Dr. Corinne Michaela Flick
Translated from German by Philippa Hurd
Layout and typesetting by Jill Sawyer Phypers
Printed and bound in Great Britain by Clays Ltd., St Ives plc

ISBN: 978-0-9931953-2-7

Previously published Convoco titles:

To Do or Not To Do—Inaction as a Form of Action (2015)

Dealing with Downturns: Strategies in Uncertain Times (2014)

Collective Law-Breaking—A Threat to Liberty (2013)

Who Owns the World's Knowledge? (2012)

**Can't Pay, Won't Pay? Sovereign Debt and the Challenge of
Growth in Europe (2011)**

"The almost insoluble task is to let neither the power of others, nor our own powerlessness, stupefy us."

—*Theodor W. Adorno (1903–69)*

CONTENTS

Introduction   1

Theses   5

1. Thoughts on the Relationship between   11
   Power and Powerlessness
   Corinne Michaela Flick

2. All Theory is Gray? Powerlessness and   19
   Power in Scientific Policy Advice
   Clemens Fuest

3. Science and Politics: Monologues, *Sermones*   43
   Absentium, or Productive Dialogue?
   Stefan Korioth

4. The Paradox of German Power and   57
   Powerlessness in Europe: A Historical
   Perspective
   Brendan Simms

5. Diplomacy and Power: On the   75
    Deployment of Military Resources
    in International Politics
    Wolfgang Ischinger

6. Who Owns the Euro? The Single   95
    Currency and National Powerlessness
    in the European Debt Crisis
    Albrecht Ritschl

7. On the Value of Companies' Political   125
    Connections
    Jörg Rocholl

8. The Power of Data and Data Quality   137
    Thomas Hoeren

9. Art, Holacracy, and the Transformation   167
    of Power Structures
    Hans Ulrich Obrist and Simon Denny

10. Thoughts on Controlling Power   187
    Christoph G. Paulus

11. The Power of the Powerless: Thoughts   201
    after Václav Havel
    Roger Scruton

    Contributors   215

INTRODUCTION

Dear Friends of Convoco,

The topic of this Convoco publication is "Power and its Paradoxes: Who's Really in Charge in a Globalized World?" We will be looking at the crossroads where politics, economics, and science intersect, and discussing expertise, advice, and—of course—influence.

Power and powerlessness always operate as a pair. They are only apparent opposites. We need to examine this combination and dependency between power and powerlessness. Our focus is on the relationship between decision-makers and advisors. Being themselves powerless, experts and advisors have nevertheless the power to influence power. If their advice is heeded, they acquire a crucial function: they give the decision-maker access to the world by highlighting the choices available. Because of this the decisions made by the decision-maker are less free. He is dependent on the advice of his advisors and experts. Thus both advisor and decision-maker are dependent on each other.

One example that illustrates the problem in the relationship between science and politics—that is advisor and advisee—is Bertolt Brecht's play *The Life of Galileo*. Galileo has discovered Jupiter's moons, and in order to please the ruling Medici family he names them the "Medici stars." With this discovery Galileo has proved the existence of the heliocentric planetary system. But the courtiers are not even willing to look through the telescope. They accuse Galileo of having painted the stars on the telescope lens. Galileo's scientific discovery threatened to undermine the structures on which power was based. This is a classic case of resisting advice.

At the same time it is important to shed light on the antechambers of power. We should acknowledge the influence advisors have, and what role their impact has, so that the democratic process is not undermined, for example, or transparency lost. The sovereign power rests with the people and so the people must be able to rely on their elected representatives not to let their experts and committees make the decisions, or even to shift responsibility onto the latter.

This book raises the questions: What is power? What does it mean to be effective today? How do we make an impact? What is the relationship between scientific advice and policy? Who has power over the Euro? How do we deal with a geopolitical loss of power? How do we limit power? How must our understanding of power change? In his essay Roger Scruton offers an answer: "True sovereignty, true freedom, true responsibility are one and the same [...]. You are not free just because you can do what you want, or satisfy your appetites. [...] It is the power that resides in truth itself, in the ability to stand before the other in open dialogue, and to recognize that he has the right to disagree."

Corinne Michaela Flick, January 2016

THESES

CORINNE M. FLICK

It is an interesting phenomenon that power does not appear alone, but is linked to powerlessness. This seems paradoxical, but only at first sight. In reality power and powerlessness are only apparent opposites. They belong together like two sides of the same coin; they are mutually dependent.

CLEMENS FUEST

At least as much as big personalities in politics and policy advice, we need excellent science, intelligible communication skills from policy advisors, and intellectual argument. Intellectual argument means that we should not see controversy and dissent in the debate as negative but as fruitful. Theory is not gray; policy advice has the power it needs. If contributions produced by policy advice lead to public contro-versy, then policy advice is working. In Germany in particular we do not need more conformism but more fruitful dissent. Ultimately the best guardian of the common good is neither politics nor policy advice, but a combative, critical, and lively public.

STEFAN KORIOTH

Science and politics have not drifted apart since 1945—quite the contrary. The awareness of interdependence has become stronger rather than weaker. One constant in this development is that today, whether it likes it or not, science is influenced more strongly by its social and political surroundings than science can conversely make its mark on them. In any event, what remains science's obligation is the preservation of its independ-ence, starting with the formulation of its questions, and ending in its attempts at answering them.

BRENDAN SIMMS

The historical record shows that successful unions have resulted not from gradual processes of conver-gence in relatively benign circumstances, but through sharp ruptures in periods of extreme crisis. They come about not through evolution but with a "big bang." They are *events* rather than *processes*. The European political unity, which the continent so desperately needs, therefore requires a single collective act of will, by its governments and elites and ultimately by its citizens.

WOLFGANG ISCHINGER

In the future, time and again conflicts will be dealt with using military power. The theory, however, that anything can be solved with overwhelming military dominance has proven to be a fallacy. People have understood—a realization that can be traced back to Clausewitz—that as a general rule only military problems can be solved by military force. But if a political problem must be solved, what is needed most of all is a political concept whose implementation might possibly require military involvement.

ALBRECHT RITSCHL

Without a solution to the problem of sovereign debt the future of the Euro is the perpetuation of the state of emergency: a Euro that is longer-lasting than we thought, more malleable than we wanted, and in which an unregulated system of fiscal transfers is binding the weak countries to the strong, whether they want it or not. As long as the debt issue in Europe remains unresolved, one thing will remain the same: the position of the ECB as the unchallenged manager of the crisis, the master of the perpetual state of emergency, and the true if extra-constitutional sovereign of the Eurozone.

JÖRG ROCHOLL

The dividing line between legitimate lobbying and reprehensible corruption is very fine, and thus it is particularly important to describe the criteria that can ensure that companies' political connections are employed in a transparent and accountable way.

THOMAS HOEREN

Power has a lot to do with knowledge, access to, and utilization of data. But in the context of the debate about power, the question of data quality is hardly ever raised. This is because legal standards for data quality are lacking.

SIMON DENNY

It's really interesting the way that people who work in supposedly secret associations such as the NSA often put all their work histories online. It's very easy, if you spend enough time, to map out a group of co-workers from the way that they're working within these institutions. The public display of things on social media undermines the secrecy of the government agency.

CHRISTOPH G. PAULUS

Beginning with the antithesis of power and powerlessness, in which the allocation of roles is by no means clear as the powerful can be powerless and vice versa, we can see that the exercise of power triggers counter-movements that try to control power. According to which power base is in question, whether it can be changed or not, the methods for controlling power are various. However, they always have the inherent characteristic that, like water in communicating vessels, they are mutually dependent.

ROGER SCRUTON

Where the ruling power has no authority, the search for authority—even if it is only a charismatic and personal authority—brings power of another kind, power that is effective in ways that the "authorities," as they ironically called themselves, could not hope to enjoy. This was the power to move people's hearts and souls, and to join with them in what Jan Patočka called "the solidarity of the shattered." It is a power that comes from placing truth where it belongs, at the center of your life, and at the beginning and end of our discourse.

CHAPTER 1

THOUGHTS ON THE RELATIONSHIP BETWEEN POWER AND POWERLESSNESS

CORINNE MICHAELA FLICK

What does it mean to be effective today?

First of all, the concept of power is neutral. Power cannot be seen as positive or negative in itself. It is only through the manner in which power is used that it becomes a force for good or for oppression.

For the sociologist Max Weber power meant "the probability that one actor within a social relationship will be in a position to carry out his own will despite resistance, regardless of the basis on which this probability rests."[1] Power is the ability to subject others to your will, that is to control the action of others. The aim is to exert control over the effect of this action,[2] as in exerting power it is primarily a question of the effectiveness of the action. Having power means achieving an effect by activating or preventing something, not just undertaking something or by acting for or against something. This notion can be found in Chinese culture above all. The philosopher Rainer Forst also understands power as the ability "to influence the justificatory space of others, or if necessary to determine (or even finalize) it."[3] Accordingly, power is the ability to motivate others to think or do something that they otherwise would not have thought or done. "[That] means that power actually operates at the level of reasons."[4] This, one could say, is where the real struggle for power takes place.

It is an interesting phenomenon that power does not appear alone, but is linked to powerlessness. This seems paradoxical, but only at first sight. In reality power and powerlessness are only apparent opposites. They belong together like two sides of the same coin; they are mutually dependent. The power to make decisions and the powerlessness to do so are always mutually related. A dialectic exists between the two. For example, a decision-maker cannot make decisions without access to the world. In many cases he gains this access via third parties, who brief and advise him before he makes a decision. Every decision comes about through the weighing up of alternatives. Margaret Thatcher's famous saying, TINA—"There Is No Alternative"—does not provide a basis for making a decision. A true decision requires at least one alternative, and in order to sift through these possibilities expertise is usually required; nowadays most decisions require relevant competence.

The tendency towards the economization of all important aspects of life intensifies this trend. In addition the tide of information to which we are exposed is a challenge that must be overcome. Increasingly the complexity of our state, economic, and social developments calls for experts and advisors to prepare decisions.

In order to fulfill the criterion of responsible opinion-making, a culture of procuring specialist knowledge is required. Such a culture has been emerging for several years.[5] An autonomous decision is less and less possible, which should not mean that one cannot make intuitive decisions. When all the alternatives are considered, one is often asked to decide for oneself intuitively.

As we have already seen, the decision-maker gains access to the world via third parties. Advisors, arbitrators, and experts are substantially involved in the decision-making process. Here we should note that a neutral advisor who does not want to exert any influence, or a rational decision-maker who decides independently and without being influenced, does not exist. Good advice means the misery of powerlessness for the decision-maker. In the most extreme case the person in power becomes a puppet of his advisors. One might say that powerlessness can be more powerful than power itself, as "he who holds a lecture before the holder of power or informs him, already has a part in power... It suffices for him to submit impressions and motives to the human individual in whose hand the decision lies for an instant."[6]

Power is regulated via access to the person in power, as it depends on being listened to. History provides us with examples, such as Cardinal Richelieu and Louis XIII, or in particular Cardinal Mazarin and Louis XIV. These two advisors usurped power. They made decisions for a child-king by having access to their mothers. In their roles as educators and counselors they themselves became powerful.

For Machiavelli, too, the problem of policy advice lay in the problem of access. As a Florentine and republican who had been banished, he had to prove himself to be a loyal advisor to the Medici, who opposed the republic. Without access one cannot instill one's advice, and one remains excluded from power. Recent history shows that experts are only listened to if they have access to power. For example, accurate predictions of the fall of communism in 1989 and the financial crisis of 2008 were made by experts who had no direct access to power and thus were not listened to. Economists such as Nouriel Roubini and the later Nobel Prize winner Robert Shiller had been predicting the financial crisis as early as 2006. In Ireland the economics professor Morgan Kelly highlighted evidence of the Irish property bubble early on, and was publicly attacked as a result. In the 1970s experts in various countries predicted the fall of communism, but as the prevailing opinion considered the USSR to be in a strong position, these findings were not seriously incorporated into policy-making.

THE RELATIONSHIP BETWEEN SCIENCE AND POLITICS

Today politicians are frequently advised by scientists. Besides the body of knowledge that science makes available, political advice contributes to the formulation of policy. The philosopher Peter Sloterdijk defines an expert as someone who draws attention to a problem, and in some cases identifies the problem for the first time. Sloterdijk sees the primary function of experts as raising people's consciousness of problems. According to him, a problem is the way in which we talk about an issue, that means how we deal with it.[7]

We can be effective through our ability to direct people's interest towards problems. This is how power is expressed. We might call this "leadership by defining problems." This means directing our attention by identifying issues. In politics, we talk about setting the agenda. People and public opinion can be influenced by leading the way in identifying topics, by owning concepts, by demonstrating competence in defining problems.[8] Science is powerful in its powerlessness. This dialectic of powerlessness and power cannot be overcome. It also shows that power is not firmly rooted in institutions or structures.

What maintains the balance between power and powerlessness? Law legitimizes power on the one hand, while controlling it on the other. A democratic legal system is a system of freedoms. It is the guarantor of people being able to live together. An essential task for the study of law is to justify a system that is acceptable and can be implemented, as the law—like religion and the philosophy of law—is the ultimate justification of a society because it gives direction. It is the fundamental, secure basis on which the individual stands.

We could say that every society is like its legal system. The stronger the law is rooted in a society, the more reliably this society functions. The law guarantees a civilized coexistence in freedom on the basis of trust.

At this point it is, therefore, important to recall the definition of "us," that is of the collective, as a society of common values, as a society of constitutional and legal patriots, as Dolf Sternberger says.[9] We should love our laws, particularly in the way in which we observe and value them, for ultimately it is the law that limits the power of the individual as it does the power of companies and governments, and protects us from the abuse of power. As Machiavelli said: "For as good customs have need of laws for maintaining themselves, so the laws, to be observed, have need of good customs."[10]

Notes

1. Max Weber, *Economy and Society: An Outline of Interpretive Sociology*, ed. Guenther Roth and Claus Wittich (Berkeley: UCal Press, 1978), p. 53.

2. Bazon Brock, *Der Barbar als Kulturheld* (Cologne: Dumont, 2002), paragraph 537.

3. Rainer Forst, *Normativität und Macht. Zur Analyse sozialer Rechtfertigungsordnungen* (Berlin: Suhrkamp, 2015), p. 22.

4. Rainer Forst, Research project "Power, Rule and Violence in Orders of Justification", http://www.normativeorders. net/en/research/projects-2012-2017/66-forschung/for-schungsprojekte-2012-2017/1329-power-rule-and-vio-lence-in-orders-of-justification (accessed December 10, 2015).

5. Cf. John Brockman, *The Third Culture* (New York: Touchstone, 1995); Carlo Strenger, *Zivilisierte Verachtung. Eine Einleitung zur Verteidigung unserer Freiheit* (Berlin: Suhrkamp, 2015), p. 99, paragraph 9.

6. Carl Schmitt, "Dialogue on Power and Access to the Holder of Power" in Carl Schmitt, *Dialogues on Power and Space*, eds. Andreas Kalyvas and Federico Finchelstein, trans. Samuel Garrett Zeitlin (Cambridge: Polity, 2015), pp. 34–5.

7. Peter Sloterdijk in conversation with Martin Walser, *Cicero* magazine, 11/2013, p. 132.

8. Cf. Brock, see note 2 above, pp. 540, 580.

9. Cf. Dolf Sternberger, "Verfassungspatriotismus" in Sternberger, *Schriften*, vol. X, *Verfassungspatriotismus* (Frankfurt: Insel Verlag, 1990), pp. 3–16 (first published in *Frankfurter Allgemeine Zeitung*, May 23, 1979, p. 1).

10. Niccolò Machiavelli, *Discourses*, book I, chapter 18: http://www.constitution.org/mac/disclivy1.htm

CHAPTER 2

ALL THEORY IS GRAY? POWERLESSNESS AND POWER IN SCIENTIFIC POLICY ADVICE

CLEMENS FUEST

1. POLICY ADVICE BETWEEN POWER AND POWERLESSNESS

Anyone who wants to be an expert in the world of policy advice will very probably sooner or later hear this phrase: "All theory is gray." What is meant is that scientists do not understand the world, policy advice is pointless, and men and women with practical experience must take matters into their own hands. This is a variation on the theme of the powerlessness of scientific policy advice: powerlessness because of inability. Only policy practitioners know how policy can be made. Scientists are too far removed from the real problems.

Many people who quote this sentence probably know that it comes from Goethe's *Faust*. But they tend to forget who says it—Mephisto, the Devil:

> All theory, my friend, is grey.
> Life's golden tree is green.[1]

Mephisto says this to a student in his study, to distract him from his books. The idea that theory is dispensable, and only practice is sufficient is thus an idea of the Devil. The Devil's ideas appear seductive at first sight, but they quickly prove to be unsustainable. One person who recognized this was John Maynard Keynes. He described the importance of theories for economic policy thus:

> Practical men who believe themselves to be quite
> exempt from any intellectual influence, are usually
> the slaves of some defunct economist.[2]

This is the thesis of the subtle power of scientific policy advice: science produces ideas. Keynes considered ideas more powerful than special interests that seem to have a great deal of influence in the short term. He thought that anyone who makes policy decisions consciously or unconsciously follows theories about the way the economy functions, theories that he has at some time heard and adopted. As Keynes was of the opinion that most people above the age of 25 to 30 stop adopting new ideas and consequently no longer alter their conceptions of state and economy, he thought that their knowledge, if they were in positions of decision-making power, was usually based on outdated ideas.[3] Dead scientists influence the economic practitioners of the following generation. Many ideas and arguments that were developed in the past are still valuable today. Some are forgotten, although they are valuable. Nevertheless, economic decisions—like policy decisions in general—should take account of current scientific findings. For this reason it would be a smart move if practitioners took an interest in modern scientific findings. Many decision-makers in the economic process indeed do this, and are at least open to a dialogue with science.

In this essay I am going to be discussing policy advice among the living. Like reflection on the subject, policy advice itself has a long history that stretches back into antiquity. In the past policy advice was often the advice given to princes, more or less authoritarian rulers. This kind of advice has its own complexity and its own contradictions.[4] In any case in important respects it is different from the policy advice of our era, that is policy advice in modern democracies, and it is to this that I would like to limit my discussion.

In recent times Germany has seen an increase in harsh criticism of policy advisors and the policy advice industry. When the German Council of Economic Experts criticized the minimum wage, many politicians wanted to abolish it immediately—not the minimum wage, but the Council. This raises the question of what contribution advice can make when those who should be advised reject the advice. Doesn't this mean that something is wrong? Rather, this dispute shows that policy advice in Germany, so long as it takes place in public, is working perfectly well.

In order to be able to comprehend this, we must understand how policy advice works in modern democracies.

2. MODELS OF POLICY ADVICE

How does policy advice work, and what can it achieve? I would like to discuss this question using a series of "models" of policy advice, that is simplified representations that bring out the essential aspects of the problem.[5]

Model 1: Advisors assert what the correct economic policy is to maximize the common good. They advise the politicians accordingly, and the politicians implement the policy.

This model of policy advice may appear naïve. However, it is very suitable as a starting point for our discussions. The model is based on a series of assumptions:

1. Such a thing as the common good exists.

2. The political decision-makers want to maximize the common good.

3. Scientists also want to maximize the common good.

4. It can be scientifically determined how the common good can be maximized.

What stands up to scrutiny in these assumptions? Assumption 1 is the least problematic, although the concept of the "common good" raises lots of questions. The idea that such a thing as "the common good" exists must not be confused with the notion that free societies have a common goal to which the members of this society must subordinate themselves. A characteristic of free societies is that their members have very different ideas about how their lives should be. The common goal is to limit individual freedoms of individual members of society only as far as necessary, so that the exercise of these freedoms does not undermine the freedom of others. In the political practice of modern democracies agreement frequently exists about certain political goals. Concerns such as the worry about internal and external security, the provision of public infrastructure, social security, environmental protection, or the promotion of science and the arts are widely accepted goals of state action.

The case of Assumption 2 is more tricky. Are political decision-makers working solely towards the maximization of the common good? If we were to vote on whether that is the case, the outcome would probably be sobering. For an economist it is anything but obvious that politicians maximize the common good. Economists work with the analytical tool of *homo oeconomicus*, who level-headedly pursues his personal interests. For politicians the pursuit above all is to remain in power, be re-elected, implement one's own ideological preferences, and perhaps acquire a large income as well.

Of course there are politicians who are idealistic and who want to increase the good of their country. But even they must make sure they are re-elected, otherwise they will not even have the opportunity of serving their country.

Thus the abovementioned Model 1 no longer pertains, and we are in Model 2 of policy advice. This can be described as follows:

Model 2: Scientists want to maximize the common good, and their work can also determine how that can happen, but politicians pursue their own interests that can deviate from the aims of the common good.

This model is only slightly more convincing than the first for reasons that we will discuss in detail shortly. However it is astonishingly widely used. I come across it in the first place in personal conversations. I am often told that it is a scandal that politics refers so little to the work of economists and does not implement their many good pieces of advice. I am frequently asked whether I am not greatly frustrated by this. I take this as a friendly gesture and assume that many of these people indeed understand that not every piece of advice from policy advisors is convincing enough to be implemented immediately.

Second, and this is more astonishing, there are scientists, who are often advisors themselves, who at least pretend to believe in this model. They continually complain that their advice is not heeded, and attribute this to politicians who are self-seeking, badly informed, or influenced by interest groups.

One example of an economist with this point of view is Jeffrey Frankel, who after all was economic advisor to US President Bill Clinton. He wrote an essay with the title "What Can an Economic Adviser Do When the President Adopts Bad Economic Policies?"[6]

In the essay he writes: "It would be a remarkable coincidence if any president accepted every position that his economic advisers had taken on every issue. But there are likely to be especially large divergences between this president and good economics in such areas as budget deficits, steel tariffs, subsidies to agriculture and other special interests, and expansionary monetary policy."[7]

This raises the question of whether Assumptions 3 and 4 in our original model apply—these are the assumptions that political advisors always aim to increase the common good, and that they know what must be done to achieve this. For an economist it is illogical to assume that all people take more notice of their own interests than the common good, and act accordingly, and that only policy advisors act in a completely selfless way.

Frankel writes that as a Harvard professor during his time as an advisor in Washington he is always also thinking that one day he will return to his professorship and have to face the criticism of his colleagues. Whoever argued for "bad" economic policy would lose face. This brings us to the question of how individual actors in the policy advice industry can perhaps be induced to work for the common good, even when they are self-interested. We shall come back to this.

First, however, we should look into the question of whether our fourth assumption does not contradict life experience: the idea that the work of experts can establish how the common good can be increased.

3. THE IMPORTANCE OF SCIENTIFIC FINDINGS AS THE BASIS OF ECONOMIC DECISIONS

When using scientific findings to underpin economic decisions, the problem arises that science cannot give unambiguous answers to many important questions.

One example is offered by research on a question that is somewhat removed from economic policy: does the death penalty work as a deterrent?[8]

This question is important, as if the death penalty does not work as a deterrent, if for example it does not reduce the number of murders, then a central argument for its justification disappears.

The question of whether the death penalty prevents crime really belongs to the realm of criminology and less to the world of economic policy. Nevertheless there is an economic approach here that concerns the creation of radical incentives. Here economic theory provides a clear hypothesis: the death penalty raises the cost of murdering for the murderer, and thus the death penalty reduces the number of murders.

How can we test this hypothesis empirically? We can compare the number of murders in states with and without the death penalty during a given period in time, or we can examine whether the number of murders in a country or a state changes after the abolition or introduction of the death penalty.

This raises various methodological problems, for example the question of the direction of causality: let's assume that we observe that in states with the death penalty more murders occur than in states without the death penalty. Let us assume, for example, that there are more murders in the USA than in Europe. At the same time the USA operates the death penalty, but Europe does not. We can interpret this observation in two different ways: on the one hand one could argue that the death penalty does not reduce the number of murders. On the other it might be that states with higher murder rates introduce or retain the death penalty to prevent the murder rate from increasing even further.

What is the response of scientific research to this question? Gebhard Kirchgässner has examined the available literature in a meta-study,[9] systematically assessing 102 research articles. He found that 87 of them came to a clear conclusion. Of these 87, 34 studies show that a deterrent effect does exist, while the other 53 studies contest this deterrent effect. If we ask which of the study's features explain its result best, the most important explanatory factor turns out, astonishingly, to be the author's subject area. Economists are far and away the most likely to come to the conclusion that deterrent effects exist. Authors from other disciplines arrive at this conclusion more rarely.

This does not mean that the experts are consciously manipulating the results. But in the selection of data and methods of measurement, it appears to be the case that many experts ultimately tend to find what they are looking for. In addition, studies that find no effects are more difficult to publish than those that do.

What can we conclude from this? In the first place one could argue that economics is not a science that allows the recognition of general rules and relationships. I would not agree. The economist Raj Chetty has recently argued that economics is in a similar position to medicine with regard to discovering general rules.[10] Medicine cannot provide exact answers to many major, very fundamental questions: what constitutes a healthy lifestyle? What accelerates or slows down the aging process? Is it more or less healthy to be slightly overweight? What is the general definition of being overweight? Different doctors have different opinions about these questions. Sound, unequivocal answers that are based on adequate science apparently do not exist. However in the case of questions with more limited scope, we can see more reliable results. Cisplatin is an effective drug in certain cases of cancer. For a long time people claimed that smoking was not bad for one's health, but now it is scientifically well established that smoking causes cancer. Many other findings in medicine are sound and have great practical use.

The situation is similar for economists, at least according to Chetty. Clear answers are difficult in the case of many fundamental questions: should the state try to combat recessions using debt-financed spending? Does high public expenditure have an influence on economic growth? Does inequality reduce growth? There are many arguments on these topics, and many studies that attempt to derive lessons for the future from historical experiences. However we cannot claim that these relationships are really clear.

It is different in cases where the effects of reforms on a large number of people are definable and identifiable. For example it is fairly convincingly documented in research into the labor market that secondary earners react more strongly to labor supply incentives such as salary increases than primary earners do. It has been clearly shown that smaller class sizes and qualified teachers have a significant impact on children's success in school. Higher income taxes lower business investments. In these areas, economic studies provide very valuable information for policy.

Nevertheless, economic advisors should not only provide policy with the results of their studies, they should also explain the assumptions on which these results are based, how reliable the results are, and what explains the fact that different studies produce different results.

However, such a request does not alter the facts that we must establish:

1. There are many questions to which science cannot supply clear answers, but it can supply information and arguments that must be assessed.

2. We must assume that neither scientists nor decision-makers in politics are saints, but have their very own preferences and interests and in this sense are never objective.

This brings us to a third model of policy advice:

Model 3: Both politicians and policy advisors pursue their own interests, their aim does not necessarily reside in maximizing the common good, and many questions are answered differently by different experts.

Does this insight mean that scientific objectivity does not exist, and that we cannot trust scientific policy advice?

4. THE IMPORTANCE OF THE PUBLIC, CRITICISM, AND COMPETITION FOR IDEAS FOR POLICY ADVICE

The insight that the results of scientific studies are influenced by interests, preferences, or the methodological perspectives of individual experts, raises the question of whether policy should relinquish the idea that such a thing as scientific objectivity exists. Karl Popper considered this conclusion to be wrong. He argued:

> It is completely erroneous to assume that the objectivity of a science depends upon the objectivity of the scientist. [...] ... the objectivity of science is not a matter for the individual scientist, but rather the social result of mutual criticism...[11]

Only the critical discussion of scientific results in the context of an expert audience and the general public can ensure that scientific policy advice acquires a certain degree of objectivity. I am often asked how it is that different economists produce such different recommendations, and whether this should not be a reason for policy to ignore economic advice altogether. My response to this is that I would find it more disturbing if all economists were always of the same opinion. Listening to and incorporating different opinions about how to solve economic problems is

precisely the precondition for good decisions. Karl
Popper goes so far as to argue that the ideal of a scientist who is completely objective and free of value judgments is mistaken:

> … we cannot rob the scientist of his partisanship
> without also robbing him of his humanity, nor can
> we suppress or destroy his value judgements without
> destroying him as a human being *and as a scientist*.
> Our motives and our purely scientific ideals, like the
> ideal of a pure search for truth, are deeply anchored
> in extra-scientific and, in part, in religious value
> judgements. The objective and "value-free" scientist
> is not the ideal scientist. Without passion we can
> achieve nothing—certainly not in pure science. The
> phrase "the *love* of truth" is no mere metaphor.[12]

This notion of an objectivity of scientific findings
that only comes about through critical discourse puts
huge demands on those who want to make scientific
results useable for practical ends. How can economic
decision-makers deal with the multiplicity of reports
coming from economic policy advice? In my opinion
they should listen to the experts and try to come up
with the broadest possible picture. They should
demand that scientists make their results intelligible.

The picture that emerges from this process will lead
to fairly clear conclusions in some individual cases. In

most cases, however, scientific findings will not be able to take away from politics the task and responsibility of making decisions under conditions of considerable uncertainty. Politicians are allowed to and should make these decisions, not because they are right or can understand and weigh up the arguments better than other people, but because and insofar as they are democratically legitimized to make the appropriate decisions.

We are all familiar with the fact that responsibility is not to be shifted onto advisors. When one is ill, one frequently experiences different doctors recommending different therapies. In the case of serious illnesses one should consult more than one doctor, but ultimately each patient himself should take responsibility for deciding on one course of action despite the limitations of his own understanding. The situation is similar in the case of economic decisions. Politicians should feel obliged to make their decisions on the basis of the best possible information, but then, however, they must take responsibility.

5. WHAT DOES ALL THIS MEAN FOR THE INSTITUTIONAL NATURE OF POLICY ADVICE?

In my opinion public debate plays an equally important role for effective policy advice in the interests of promoting the common good as advice that excludes the public, and which naturally also has its place.

Public discussion about political decisions, combined with pressure of elections, ensures that politicians, although they pursue their own interests, ultimately ascribe importance to the common good when making their decisions. Of course this does not work perfectly.

Georg Milbrath, himself both a politician and a scientist, recently said: "In elections it is not crucial what reality is, but rather what the electors think is real."[13]

Anyone making policy advice should understand how public debate influences perception. Here's an example. I recently demanded that if the German Bundestag wanted to sanction a new aid program for Greece, it should be linked to a decision about how the whole thing was to be financed.

If it is correct that Greece is already over-indebted, more loans are not loans but gifts of money. As this money will not fall from the skies, sooner or later there must be tax increases or spending cuts in Germany. I gave the example that to finance this aid package the solidarity surcharge could be raised from 5.5 to 8%.

This unleashed a public storm of indignation, although it is actually a very small thing to say that transfers to Greece, if they are paid, mean higher taxes or lower spending at some point in time. In the federal press conference the German government had to deny that it wants to raise taxes. I made this suggestion public as my aim was to arouse the public themselves. The great indignation and fuss that this caused demonstrates my view that the public does not always correctly understand the reality.

Whether one regards my contribution as a successful or failed form of policy advice is surely a matter of opinion. In any case this example underlines the great importance of the public for effective policy advice. In this sense policy advice is also advice given to the public, the electorate.

For this reason I think that independent policy advice is important and must be preserved. As I said at the outset, in Germany at the moment it is more and more frequently discussed whether we need an independent Council of Experts or independent advisory committees in the Federal Ministry for Economic Affairs or the Ministry of Finance. Often the government does not follow the advice of independent advisors. Replacing them with dependent advisors who make their recommendations behind closed doors would be a big mistake. Of course, dependent advisors exist: we have very capable economists in the ministries and in the Federal Chancellery. This kind of advice is important. It alone, however, cannot ensure that policy advice in a democracy, where public debate has a central importance, works perfectly in the interests of promoting the common good. Independent policy advice that is engaged with the public must play an additional role here.

6. THE ROLE OF CHARISMATIC POLITICIANS

I began with Goethe, and I would like to end with Schiller—not Friedrich Schiller, but rather Karl Schiller. He is of interest for our topic as he was a scientist who went into politics himself. He had a major impact on German economic policy of the 1960s and early 1970s.

Schiller was not a conformist politician, but a striking thinker such as is often felt to be lacking in politics today. On the subject of Schiller it was written that he may have been brilliant but he was also vain and arrogant. In addition he was completely resistant to advice.[14]

Even the later "world-class economist" Helmut Schmidt was not spared Karl Schiller's arrogance: as Schiller, the "super minister," said in a 1972 cabinet meeting, he could of course explain it again "but the Defense Minister [Schmidt] hadn't understood it even back then in his advanced seminar."[15]

Apparently, that is how he gave Helmut Schmidt a dressing down.

However Schiller was an extraordinary character, who perhaps is not typical of the opportunist politician that I have described here. Wilhelm Hanker said of him: "In economic policy matters there was absolutely no party line, only the scientific line. He was a professor through and through. The Group then had to be whipped into shape."[16]

Ultimately, Schiller had to resign. In his resignation letter he demanded: "It is the government's duty to look beyond election dates and tell the people in a timely manner what can be accomplished and what is demanded."[17]

Today many people long for spiky, charismatic characters such as Karl Schiller. I agree with that, but would emphasize nevertheless that we should not design our institutions in policy advice in such a way that we are dependent on the goodwill and vision of big personalities. Karl Schiller's economic policy was by no means beyond all doubt. Whether it was good for Germany is a topic that will be discussed for a long time to come.

At least as much as big personalities in politics and policy advice we need excellent science, intelligible communication skills from policy advisors and intellectual argument. Intellectual argument means that we should not see controversy and dissent in the debate as negative but as fruitful.

At the same time we need politicians who understand the process of policy advice, who regard dissent and public criticism as productive, and who are open with regard to both public debate and advice given behind closed doors.

Theory is not gray; policy advice has the power it needs. If contributions produced by policy advice lead to public controversy, then policy advice is working. In Germany in particular we do not need more conformism but more fruitful dissent.

Ultimately, the best guardian of the common good is neither politics nor policy advice, but a combative, critical, and lively public.

Notes

1. Johann Wolfgang von Goethe, *Faust, Part I*, trans. David Constantine (London: Penguin Classics, 2005), p. 68.

2. John Maynard Keynes, *The General Theory of Employment, Interest, an Money* (New York: Snowball Publishing, 2012 [1936]), p. 383.

3. "… in the field of economic and political philosophy there are not many who are influenced by new theories after they are twenty-five or thirty years of age, so that the ideas which civil servants and politicians and even agitators apply to current events are not likely to be the newest. But, soon or late, it is ideas, not vested interests, which are dangerous for good or evil." Keynes, *General Theory*, p. 382.

4. See Felix Wassermann, "Die Paradoxie des Rats. Niccolò Machiavelli und Thomas Morus über und als politische Berater" in Harald Bluhm, Karsten Fischer and Marcus Llanque (eds.), *I eenpolitik. Geschichtliche Konstellationen un gegenwärtige Konflikte* (Berlin: Akademie Verlag, 2011), pp. 563–86.

5. On the following ideas cf. Gebhard Kirchgässner, "Zur Rolle der Ökonometrie in der wissenschaftlichen Politikberatung" in *Perspektiven er Wirtschaftspolitik* 14 (2013), pp. 3–30.

6. Jeffrey Frankel, "What Can an Economic Adviser do when the President adopts Bad Economic Policies?" The Pierson Lecture, Swarthmore, April 21, 2005.

7. Frankel, "What Can an Economic Advisor Do," p. 3.

8. Kirchgässner, "Zur Rolle der Ökonometrie."

9. Cf. Berit C. Gerritzen and Gebhard Kirchgässner, "Facts or Ideology: What Determines the Results of Econometric Estimates of the Deterrence Effect of Death Penalty?" CESifo Working Paper 4159, March 2013, Munich.

10. Cf. Raj Chetty, "Yes, Economics is a Science" in *New York Times*, October 20, 2013. http://www.nytimes.com/2013/10/21/opinion/yes-economics-is-a-science.html

11. Karl Popper, "The Logic of the Social Sciences" in *In Search of a Better World: Lectures and Essays from Thirty Years*, trans. Laura J. Bennett with additional material by Melitta Mew (London/New York: Routledge, 1994), p. 72.

12. Popper, "The Logic", p. 74.

13. Said during a platform discussion held on the occasion of the 2015 annual meeting of the Munich ifo Institute.

14. Cf. Jörg Lichter, *Handelsblatt*, December 7, 2007.

15 Ibid.

16. Quoted in Matthias Hochstätter, "Karl Schiller – eine wirtschaftspolitische Biographie," diss., University of Hanover (2006), p. 294.

17. Quoted in Hochstätter "Karl Schiller," p. 298.

CHAPTER 3

SCIENCE AND POLITICS: MONOLOGUES, SERMONES ABSENTIUM, OR PRODUCTIVE DIALOGUE?

STEFAN KORIOTH

How do science and politics interact? Have they become distant from each other over the last few decades? Can political processes bypass scientific discoveries? Can science occupy a politics-free zone? I want to answer these questions concisely in light of the relationship between both areas since 1945. During this period we can identify four phases in the changeable relationship between politics and science, phases that are not characterized by clear-cut caesuras but which overlap. In this essay the concepts of politics and science should be thought of very broadly but related to their subject areas. Even one hundred years on, the classifications by Max Weber, an author who himself saw both areas as some distance apart, are still helpful. For Weber politics is related to influencing an association, in particular the state, and is to do with "the distribution or preservation of power, or a shift in power." "Whoever is active in politics strives for power, either power as a means in the service of other goals, whether idealistic or selfish, or power 'for its own sake', in other words, so as to enjoy the feeling of prestige that it confers."[1] Science, on the other hand, based on the process of further rationalizing and intellectualizing the world, is a collaborative operation, a "profession practiced in specialist *isciplines*" in the "service of reflection on the self and the knowledge of relationships between facts and not a gift of grace on the part of seers and prophets dispensing sacred goods and revelations. Nor is it part of the meditations of sages and philosophers about the *meaning* of the world."[2]

I.

The first phase of the more recent relationship between politics and science extends from 1945 to around 1960. Its starting point is on the one hand the rapid development of the sciences since 1900,[3] in particular the natural sciences, and on the other hand the clear, global partitioning of the centers of political power as a result of World War II. For the most part science and scientists display a surprisingly naïve attitude towards politics. There is a widespread, unquestioning notion that scientists operate in a politics-free zone and are free to decide whether scientific discoveries should be made accessible to politics. Politics' particular interest in exploiting the natural sciences to increase power encounters science's willingness to make discoveries available for reasons of patriotism, vanity, and even for the pleasure of seeing their discoveries put into practice. The paradigm of this is how the peaceful and non-peaceful use of nuclear fission was handled. The dropping of the atom bomb in August 1945 has at its core one of the shortest and simplest routes from basic research to (military) politics that has ever existed in the history of humanity. The enormous potential of the invention is well known and is happily passed on. Politics hardly needs to deploy its own instruments of power to acquire this knowledge. The massive political returns entail consequences: "But today the dangerousness of the technical means has escalated boundlessly. Consequently the dangerousness of humans to other humans has correspondingly escalated as well. As a result the distinction between power and powerlessness is growing in such a boundless way, that it is drawing the concept of the human itself into fully new modes of questioning."[4] A broader debate about responsibility for the exploitation of basic research only starts in the second half of the 1950s, encouraged in no small part by plays such as Friedrich Dürrenmatt's *The Physicists* and Heinar Kipphardt's *In the Matter of J. Robert Oppenheimer.* There is another important factor in this first phase. During this period the social sciences play a strikingly secondary role. Nevertheless, innovative developments in sociology, economics, and law raise the question of how human behavior can be stabilized in societies in order to prevent catastrophes such as those seen in the first half of the century. However it is also striking that many social scientists look enviously at the natural sciences and lament that they cannot offer politics any important useable findings—in the 1950s many even think that with the juxtaposition of the two systems of democratically controlled capitalism and democratic socialism the most sophisticated human social systems imaginable have been reached, and that they cannot be surpassed.

II.

The second phase extends until around the end of the 1960s. Meanwhile science knows which keys to power and for power it holds, and that it has to bear a scientific, ethical, and social responsibility for handing over this key. Politics adapts to the new cautiousness and responsibility of science. To some extent they are respected, but to another extent politics tries to influence science with its formal and informal instruments of power, by controlling science policy, and not least by the targeted distribution and withholding of resources. This is all the more effective as major research programs are not independently financially viable and rely on long-term and dependable funding from the public purse. Occasionally this leads to cynicism in science that finds itself in a friendly but also inescapable embrace with political power. Uwe Johnson describes this in the first volume of his *Anniversaries* series, using the example of "D.E.", the well-paid physicist who, after university, escapes the GDR to work on secret weapons projects in the USA: "An occasion involving moral issues was one of the few times D.E. almost blew up. [...] In his opinion, morality is the business of the administrators of power who proclaim it, and not the concern of their dependents, whose business is survival. A man who does not work visibly in defense, even if only in the bakery of his army camp, is working for defense; the difference is purely subjective, objectively trifling." The physicists trusted "with wonderful certainty that none of them will ever be treated as a war criminal and each of them will be considered a specialist; this removes any inhibitions."[5]

However as a whole a comparatively peaceful and productive exchange emerges between the two spheres, occasionally even a symbiosis. Humankind is still in thrall to the belief in almost continuous progress. The slogan is the all-encompassing "scientification" of society, to be joined later by the "socialization" of science, even its "democratization." Advisory committees and seminars populated with experts appear everywhere, while rational planning, the "cybernetics" of social processes as well, is the order of the day. In Germany concepts emerge based on sociology, law, and economics such as Karl Schiller's "concerted action" and the "formed society" (coined by Rüdiger Altmann working as an advisor to Ludwig Erhard), and the "general management" of economic processes by the guiding hand of the public sector is derived directly from the then new economic ideas. Not least, all this plays out in the context of the ubiquitous competition between the systems of East and West. While theoretical Marxism and real-life socialism both have an innate tendency to see laws and "legalities" everywhere that must be recognized and managed, now even the capitalist West does not want to lag behind.

III.

The third phase, marked by increasing disillusionment on both sides, lasts until around the end of the 1980s. It is characterized by profound changes that affect and change the premises of the relationship between science and politics. First, accompanied by shrill tales of decline particularly from conservative thinkers, the equation of state politics with the center of gravity of power is dissolved.[6] The loss of the state monopoly on power takes on very different guises: increasing international interconnectedness and dependency (for which the word "globalization" is still largely unknown), ever-closer European integration, but also "liberation movements" in the Third World, and international terrorism. However above all there is the appearance of previously unknown, transnational, private power complexes—companies that to some extent bring together characteristics that were previously the preserve of state and science as clearly separate spheres. These—primarily American[7]— companies exercise social power and increase this power not only through market competition. They also maintain their own research departments and use them to build a twofold intimacy with science and politics. In the era of the "technical realization" (Ernst Forsthoff) of what is possible, the traditional system models of state, culture, society, economy, and science begin to falter. Financial returns can be the aim of research. In addition the belief in progress and its manageability suffers considerable setbacks. Despite global management and concerted action, there are economic crises and mass unemployment; at the end of this phase Chernobyl stands for the ultimate collapse of any belief in the mastery of nature. Interestingly, during this phase, science frequently retreats to its familiar field of analysis, to suggestions for at least understanding and categorizing the given. However, even this meets with less and less success. In the name of postmodernity even science loses its belief in halfway certain knowledge and its own cognitive authority. There remains the uncertain "risk society"[8] and its "risky" specifications.

IV.

If uncertainty also causes gaps to open up, then it is clear that forces will realign to fill the gaps once again. First and above all, since the 1990s, despite the general loss of management opportunities, politics has tried to implement clear forms of hierarchy in individual areas. These areas include science in the shape of scientific organizations. Globally, science has been strongly offered and forced to accept things that originate in the alien operating conditions of politics and economics. Bureaucracy, economic models, and hierarchies increase, and research is managed through the allocation of resources more openly than before. In Germany, for example, this means that since the end of the 1990s the ongoing and secure funding of universities by the public purse has stagnated, and researchers are directed towards competition for other resources, in particular so-called "external funding." This creates new dependencies, which are manifested most clearly in science in the increasing loss of focus on basic research in favor of a focus on practical application.

STEFAN KORIOTH

Scientific knowledge is and should no longer be acquired in isolation and freedom, at a distance from the issues and interests of society. Instead basic research is bound up with applied research and practical contexts. To describe this the science of science has coined the concept of "solutionism," meaning short- to medium-term solutions for problems that are identified by others—politics and economics in particular. This also reflects the increasing impatience of the political sphere, which did not want to be stretched by a plurality of approaches—by "science in a free society."[9] Politics complains that it makes available lots of money for research on climate change, on medical and social epidemics, on biotechnology, and on saving the Euro, without getting any straightforward solutions. There is another phenomenon concerning the new distribution of power between politics and science, namely the increasing importance of committees who exercise political functions with scientific expertise or combine the latter with social interests. An example of this is the increasing number and importance of ethics committees that now exist in numerous institutions to give policy advice, in healthcare providers, or in scientific institutions themselves. This applies not only at national level, but also in the European Union. This development has both positive and negative effects: whether intentionally or unintentionally ethics committees curtail public debates and make them less democratic. However they also set limits for science in the interest of social or ethical values or ideals. Research involving experimentation on animals is put up against animal protection as a reason for abolition, a situation that previously would have been almost inconceivable.

V.

Science and politics have not drifted apart since 1945—quite the contrary. The awareness of interdependence has become stronger rather than weaker. One constant in this development is that today, whether it likes it or not, science is influenced more strongly by its social and political surroundings than science can conversely make its mark on them. In any event, what remains science's obligation is the preservation of its independence, starting with the formulation of its questions, and ending in its attempts at answering them. But the last 70 years also show the extremely wide variety of tense relationships between science and politics. At the moment the situation seems to be one of mutual dissatisfaction. However, this can be overcome by each sphere thinking through how the other functions. Anyone in science who thinks they have a good idea and is amazed when politics does not take it up, can be accused of a certain amount of naïveté. What is more, in the words of Friedrich Dürrenmatt in his "21 points to the physicists": "The more people proceed according to a plan, the more effectively they can be struck by accident." On the other hand the accusation of naïveté can also be leveled against politics if it hopes it can shift decision-making and responsibility on to the experts, and if at the same time it complains that science criticizes political processes for being volatile, lacking in logic, and short-termist. Perhaps another quotation from Dürrenmatt's 21 points can help us here: "The content of physics concerns physicists, the effects concern all of us. What concerns all of us can only be solved by all of us. Any attempt by an individual to solve a problem that concerns all of us is bound to fail." Modern societies are fully rationalized, science-based, technological cultures. This makes them both strong and weak. Inevitably, however, every area of life, even politics, is dependent on science.

Notes

1. Max Weber, "Politics as a Vocation" (1917) in Max Weber, *The Vocation Lectures*, ed. with an Introduction by David Owen and Tracy B. Strong, trans. Rodney Livingstone (Indianapolis/Cambridge: Hackett Publishing Company, 2004), pp. 33–4.

2. Max Weber, "Science as a Vocation" (1919) in Max Weber, *The Vocation Lectures*, ed. with an Introduction by David Owen and Tracy B. Strong, trans. Rodney Livingstone (Indianapolis/Cambridge: Hackett Publishing Company, 2004), p. 27.

3. This concerns not only the scope of available knowledge, but also the organization of science. Early on Helmut Plessner spoke of the "industrialization of science." See "Zur Soziologie der modernen Forschung und ihrer Organisation in der deutschen Universität – Tradition und Ideologie" (1924) in Helmut Plessner, *Diesseits der Utopie* (Frankfurt: Suhrkamp, 1974), p. 130.

4. Carl Schmitt, "Dialogue on Power and Access to the Holder of Power" in Carl Schmitt, *Dialogues on Power and Space*, eds. Federico Finchelstein and Andreas Kalyvas, trans. Samuel Garrett Zeitlin (Cambridge: Polity, 2015), p. 26.

5. Uwe Johnson, *Anniversaries. From the Life of Gesine Cresspahl*, trans. Leila Vennewitz (New York: Harcourt Brace Jovanovich, 1975), chapter of November 22, 1967, Wednesday, pp. 227–8.

6. Once again Carl Schmitt, Foreword to *Der Begriff des Politischen* [*The Concept of the Political*] (Berlin: Duncker und Humblot, 1963), "Die Epoche der Staatlichkeit geht jetzt zu Ende. Darüber ist kein Wort mehr zu verlieren" ["The era of statehood is now dying. No additional word is needed in this regard"], p. 10.

7. A frequent source is Jean-Jacques Servan-Schreiber, *The American Challenge*, trans. Ronald Steel (New York: Atheneum, 1969), above all the thesis that: "Fifteen years from now it is quite possible that the world's third greatest industrial power, just after the United States and Russia, will not be Europe, but *American industry in Europe*," p. 3.

8. Ulrich Beck, *Risk Society: Towards a New Modernity* (London: Sage, 1992).

9. The title of philosopher of science Paul Feyerabend's 1979 book (original German title: *Erkenntnis für freie Menschen* [*Knowledge for Free People*]). Feyerabend demanded not only that scientists should transgress and overstep acknowledged methodological rules deliberately and for specific reasons, but he also, interestingly, called for a clear distinction between state and science.

CHAPTER 4

THE PARADOX OF GERMAN POWER
AND POWERLESSNESS IN EUROPE: A
HISTORICAL PERSPECTIVE [1]

BRENDAN SIMMS

In his blistering speech to the Greek parliament, the former finance minister Yannis Varoufakis referred to the harsh "bailout" conditions imposed by the Eurozone leaders, and especially Berlin, as a new "Versailles." This calculated allusion to the punitive peace inflicted on imperial Germany after World War I, especially the "reparations" she was forced to pay, was picked up by media commentators and politicians across the world. Berlin's approach was widely condemned as "brutal." "The man with the gun," London's mayor Boris Johnson claims, "is the German finance minister Wolfgang Schäuble" and "it is the Germans who are now running the show." So has the Euro crisis brought about peacefully something that the Kaiser and Hitler failed to achieve militarily, namely the German domination of Europe? Less hyperbolically, was the eminent sociologist, the late Ulrich Beck, right to claim that the German Chancellor, Angela Merkel, is a calculating "Merkiavelli" whose ambition is to "Germanize" Europe?

The short answer to these questions is no. Germany is not oppressing the Greeks or any other Eurozone country. Nobody forced these previously sovereign states into the common currency, at the barrel of a gun or in any other way. It was a dance they insisted on joining, in some cases rather like the ugly stepsisters, doing violence to their real economic body shape in order to fit into the shoes of the required economic convergence criteria. Besides, none of them want to leave either the European Union or the Euro because they have no desire to return to the failed national politics they were trying to escape through "Europe." Polls suggest that, offered a clear choice between return to the drachma and reclaiming national sovereignty, or accepting German leadership of the Eurozone, the vast majority of Greeks prefer the latter. The same is true, more or less, of the rest of the common currency area. Clearly, there is only one thing worse than being dominated by Germany in the Eurozone and that is not being dominated by Germany in the Eurozone. Whatever else is going on here, it is not the recreation of the Second or Third Reich.

That said, the current crisis is very much a product of the German problem, and indeed of the German imperial legacy. In order to understand why, we need to go back to the origins of a question which has driven the history of our continent for hundreds of years and fundamentally shapes its politics today. Germany, or the various polities in which most Germans lived, has been the fulcrum of the entire European state system since at least the 16th century. Its central geographical location made it the cockpit of Europe, a territory on which foreign armies—Ottoman Turk, Spanish, French, British, Russian, French, Swedish, to name only the most prominent—contested for mastery of the continent. Its sheer populousness, the industriousness of its inhabitants, and the prowess of its soldiers, made Germany the most valued prize in the state system. "Germany," to quote the Swedish negotiator Johan Adler Salvius, was "a temperate and populous part of the world and a warlike people... there was not a country under the sun in a better position to establish a universal monarchy and absolute dominion in

Europe, than Germany... if one potentate wielded absolute power in this realm, all the neighboring realms would have to apprehend being subjugated."

For much of the past five hundred years, the fear was not that Germany itself would disturb the European balance of power but that an outside force would use the Germans to do so. This was because their political commonwealth, the "Holy Roman Empire of the German Nation," was bitterly divided between emperor and the major princes, and between Catholics and Protestants. This created a vacuum at the heart of Europe which exported instability and attracted the predatory attention of its neighbors, most catastrophically during the Thirty Years War, but also during the Turkish invasions of Central Europe and the Revolutionary and Napoleonic Wars.

For this reason, European statesmen tried to refashion Germany in such a way that the Germans were not always at each other's throats, or at the feet of their neighbors. This required institutions that defused internal tensions, if necessary through outside intervention, and mobilized common energies in defense of the Empire's external borders. German politics were therefore characterized by a sophisticated form of power-sharing through imperial courts and the imperial assembly, the Reichstag. France and Sweden were guarantor powers from the Peace of Westphalia in 1648, with the right to intervene in German affairs to keep the peace or to prevent foreign interference, and in the 18th century Russia was also formally awarded that privilege. The German Confederation of 1815, the successor to the Empire, was constructed on very similar lines in order to ensure that Germany did not lapse into civil war and remained strong enough to repel outside invaders, but never became so strong as to pose a threat to its neighbors.

The result was a German political culture preoccupied with precedents, legality, rules, and procedure to the point of paralysis. Due to the failure of the Empire to mobilize effectively against the Ottoman Turks in the 16th and 17th centuries, and against the French in the 17th and 18th centuries, the Germans themselves were well aware of their weaknesses, and tried vainly to overcome them through an interminable and ultimately ineffectual "Imperial Reform Debate." After a long agony, however, the Holy Roman Empire collapsed under the onslaught of Revolutionary France and Napoleon. Later, the German Confederation, which failed to deter French revanchism, was destroyed by Bismarck and the National Liberals in their drive to create a united Germany. This turned the Germans from objects of the state system into subjects, with a powerful voice in Europe and the world.

The new United Germany was by any standard a colossus. With a population of 41 million people, it was larger than France (36 million), Austria-Hungary (35.8 million) and Britain (31 million). Only the vast Tsarist Empire could boast an even greater number of subjects (77 million).[2] By comparison, the population of Prussia in 1850 had been 16 million. Moreover, unlike its stagnating French rival, the German population was rapidly increasing. Harnessed to this demographic motor was a rapidly industrializing economy, the best educational system in the world, and of course an army which was second to none. This vast new entity was located at the heart of Europe. The consolidation of the European center, largely complete by 1866, had now become a permanent fixture. Where there had for hundreds of years been a plethora of smaller states, and as recently as seven years previously there had still been nearly 40 distinct entities, a single power ruled supreme.

As is well known, however, the establishment of a consolidated power center at the heart of the continent eventually overturned the whole European and ultimately the global balance of power. It required a coalition of the world's strongest powers to crush both the

Kaiser's Germany and Hitler's Third Reich in the two world wars. These events showed Germany's great strength but also her weakness. True, she was able to defy much of the world for four years in 1914–18, and another six years in 1939–45, but in the end she failed. This in spite of the fact that Germany controlled much of Central and Eastern Europe in World War I and almost all of continental Europe in World War II. Integration of Europe by German domination did not work. In short, Germany's position was, as the historian Ludwig Dehio put it memorably, "semi-hegemonial," or in Henry Kissinger's no less inspired words, "Germany was too big for Europe but too small for the world." The paradox of German power and powerlessness could not have been better expressed.

After each contest, the German question posed itself anew: how to order the European center in such a way that it was robust enough to master domestic and external challenges without at the same time developing hegemonic tendencies. The Versailles Settlement spectacularly failed to do so, primarily because it was resented as an attempt to turn Germans back into mere objects of the state system.

The solution arrived at after World War II was far more enduring. Germany was partitioned territorially into a communist East and a democratic West, and underwent a change of heart internally. It was widely accepted that what was needed, as the writer Thomas Mann argued, was not a "German Europe" but a "European Germany." The project of European integration was thus intended to contain Germany by rendering her structurally incapable of and culturally indisposed towards military aggression. It was also conceived as a way of mobilizing Europe's, and especially Germany's, huge military and economic potential for the western cause against the Soviet threat. The reintegration of Germany into the western comity of nations, including the generous forgiveness of many of her debts at the 1953 London Agreement, was conducted on this basis.

But while pacifying Europe, and containing Germany, required a European constitutional arrangement and political culture similar to the old Holy Roman Empire, keeping the Russians out demanded a mighty union comparable to that created by the British and the Americans. On the one hand, the growing strain of containing the Soviet Union made it imperative that the Western Europeans do more for their own defense, either collectively or individually, for example through German rearmament. On the other hand, the European Coal and Steel Community, which established a joint administration of French and German coal and steel resources, was ostensibly a form of economic rationalization, but really a device to bring the war-making potential of Germany under multilateral control and thus de-fang her.

As Germany's industry recovered there were growing fears in Paris and elsewhere in Europe that the mighty Deutschmark, which gave the Bundesbank effective control over European interest rates, constituted a kind of German "nuclear weapon." Even before German unification was on the agenda, the French President François Mitterrand warned that "[w]ithout a common currency we are... already subordinate to the Germans' will." At the Madrid Summit of the European council in June 1989 the Euro was finally agreed, before communism collapsed but firmly within a context of the growth of German power in Europe. When the Berlin Wall fell in November 1989 the process of introducing a currency union gained new urgency. France rejoiced as the Deutschmark was decommissioned, with some commentators openly describing the settlement, ironically in view of Mr. Varoufakis's later remarks, as a new "Versailles." "Germany will pay," they crowed, echoing another slogan from 1919. A veritable torrent of cheap credit, uncorked by the Euro and the reduced sense of sovereign debt risk it engendered, now slowly began to engulf the continent, especially its southern and western periphery.

Currency union was not accompanied by full political union, however. The EU retained its loose confederal governance structure. The French believed that they had neutralized the German economic threat, while retaining their political sovereignty and military autonomy. They effectively uncoupled political and economic union, hoping that one could have a European solution for the economy, where Germany was strong, and a French solution for foreign policy and defense, where the French imagined themselves more powerful.

This political halfway house was not what Chancellor Kohl had intended, but it suited his compatriots perfectly well. They uploaded much of their premodern political culture into the EU, especially a penchant for the juridification of political disputes, interminable debate, and due process, so that the EU began increasingly to resemble the old Holy Roman Empire. The French Interior Minister and sometime Defense Minister Jean-Pierre Chevènement even accused the Germans of trying to dilute the power of the national states, and thus the barriers to their dominance, by holding up the Holy Roman Empire as a model for European constitutional development.

He was only half right, in the sense that much of the authority lost by the Member States in the crucial areas of fiscal, foreign, and military policy was not so much arrogated as atomized. Like the old Empire, the European Union was based on the diffusion rather than the concentration of power. In strategic terms, the EU takes the immense economic, demographic and military potential of the continent and reduces it.

This did not much bother Germans, especially after the collapse of communism, because the expansion of the EU and NATO eastwards meant that Germany was, for the first time in her long history, surrounded only by friends; her interest in security matters, especially the problem of Russian power, began to lapse. When Mr. Putin began to use energy as a weapon against its neighbors, Germans pushed ahead with the North Stream pipeline which sheltered them from any fallout resulting from supply disputes concerning Poland and Ukraine. Indeed, rather than attempting to throw its weight about in Europe militarily after the fall of the Wall, as many had predicted, Germany refused to participate in the first Gulf War, and only involved herself in the subsequent Yugoslav Wars and the War on Terror within a firmly multilateral framework. One way or the other, it seemed, the German behavioral transformation since 1945 had neutralized the structural shift wrought by reunification. The German Question, it appeared, had been solved by Germany's integration into the West.

In behavioral terms, this was perfectly true. The Germans had indeed changed, but Europe had not, or not enough. First, the German economy recovered: the talk was of a new *Mo₁ell Deutschlan₁*. Then the bubble caused by currency union on the western and southern periphery exploded, and in the absence of political union, Europe found itself without the necessary instruments to respond beyond national level. The confederal political structure of the currency union favored its largest member. As the largest and most healthy economy, Germany was not only well placed to weather the storm, but increasingly dominated the pan-European response. It was reluctant to empower the European Central Bank to embark on the bond-buying mission the bankrupt European periphery so desperately craves, and has prescribed them a diet of unpalatable fiscal "rules" instead.

Then the European security bubble exploded. In March 2014, Russian aggression in Ukraine raised the question of the extent to which the Germans, snug in their Central European idyll, far from the epicenter of the crisis, desirous of good trading relations with Moscow, and thirsting for Russian energy, were capable of thinking of the general geopolitical good of Europe, now that their own immediate security no longer seemed to depend on it. Yet their disengagement was no more selfish than that of, say, the even more remote Spaniards and Italians, and it was not only enabled but facilitated by the ineffectual political design of the Union, which has dissipated the vast economic and military potential of the continent rather than bringing it to bear on the common enemy. To make matters worse still, Europe was convulsed by a migrant crisis in the summer and autumn of 2015, during which Angela Merkel's unilateral offer of asylum in Germany threatened to destabilize the Schengen Agreement and caused widespread consternation, especially in Eastern and Southeastern Europe.

In short, the current mess is not primarily the fault of the Germans specifically, but of the German problem, which is not the same thing. As we have seen, European integration was designed both to contain and mobilize Germany, most recently through the Euro, but the unwillingness of the rest of Europe to enter into a matching full political union meant that the EU faced the resulting sovereign debt crisis and the Russian challenge without the necessary governmental apparatus to end the crisis. Moreover, the European project as currently constructed, and especially the currency union, originally designed to contain German power, has actually increased it. Germany is not more to blame for this situation than anybody else in the Eurozone.

So the German question has mutated over more than half a millennium. For four hundred years or so, Germany was too weak. The question was how to mobilize the Germans in defense of the balance of power, or to prevent them from falling into the hands of a hegemon. For about 80 years after unification in 1871, Germany was too strong, and either threatened world peace or appeared to do so. Then followed about half a century in which Germany was relatively weak in political terms, and contributed far less to the western cause than it could have done. Today, as we have seen, Germany is both too strong and too weak, or at least too disengaged. Her austerity policies and her unilateralism in the refugee question suggest an excess of German power to critics, while her strategic weakness in the face of Russian aggression and state breakdown in the Middle East seem to suggest the absence of power, or at least of a sense of responsibility.

To be sure, critics are right to source much of the current European malaise in the German imperial legacy, but the empire in question is not that of the Kaiser or Hitler but the old Holy Roman Empire whose strengths and weaknesses live on in the European Union of today. Instead of anchoring the common currency in a joint parliamentary representation and a strong state capable of efficient revenue extraction, as is the case in the United Kingdom and the United States, Berlin is attempting to run it through the acceptance of German "rules" and political culture. Instead of a single foreign policy and military capable of deterring aggressors, we have a perpetual palaver which reminds one of nothing so much as the vacillations of the Holy Roman Empire in the face of Turkish or French threats.

Whatever the solution, it will have to allow the Germans to continue to act as subjects of the European system, without turning most other peoples on the continent into objects. It will have to avoid a "Versailles" for both Germany and everybody else. It will also have to mobilize the collective energies of Europe, including those of Germany, to deal with the enormous challenges posed by the growth of Russia's power, and to compensate for the relative decline of the United States. It will have to close the gap that opened up between politico-military and socioeconomic integration in Europe in the 1950s. In short, it must once and for all settle the German and European questions in one stroke, for to settle the one is to settle the other.[3]

There is a way forward. It must begin with a return to grand strategic thinking, something which has been almost entirely neglected for many decades on this side of the Atlantic, with some honorable exceptions (e.g. Robert Cooper). We have heard too much recently about globalization, interdependence, and the resulting irrelevance of the classic themes of diplomacy. In fact, the main external challenges facing us in Europe today—from Russian territorial revisionism and the Islamist caliphate in the Middle East— are very similar to those of past centuries. The main internal question, which is how to design a state in which currency, debt, and parliamentary representation can be reconciled, has been addressed and solved in the past. It is with these thoughts in mind that my collaborators and I have established a Forum on Geopolitics at Cambridge, which I hope to grow into a full-scale Centre for Geopolitics before too long. One of our programs is the "Laboratories for World Construction," in which we try to explore historically based solutions to real-world problems, for example the German Question and the European problem.

Our work there feeds into my other practical initiative, which is the "Project for Democratic Union."

This is a start-up think-tank, established by myself and some students and young professionals a few years ago, which has a presence in several other European cities. While it is still a small outfit for now, I am confident that it can grow to be one of the most important voices on the future of the Eurozone, and indeed Europe in the future. Our aim is to create a politically unified Eurozone on Anglo-American constitutional lines, either with the United Kingdom or in close confederation with it. A book due to be published in 2016 together with the Director of the PDU, Benjamin Zeeb, sets out our program under the somewhat provocative title: *Europa schafft sich ab* (Europe is abolishing itself).

Our solution, developed by the Forum on Geopolitics and the PDU, involves Germans and Europeans abandoning the loose traditions of the old Reich and its successor, the European Union, and turning instead to the example of the Anglo-American democracies of the West, where similar problems have been addressed and mastered in the past.

In the early 18th century, the English and Scots brought hundreds of years of military, diplomatic and economic rivalry to an end by joining forces. The aim of the Anglo-Scottish Union was twofold: first, to bring to an end the longstanding rivalry between the two states, which had given England's enemies a regular opportunity to put pressure on her northern border; second, to mobilize the joint resources more effectively against outside powers, rather than dissipating them through commercial and colonial competition. The resulting Act of Union (1707), in which Scotland received generous representation at Westminster, retained its legal and educational system, but gave up its separate foreign and security policy.[4] Great Britain was born, and with it a fiscal–military state which has punched above its "natural" weight in the world ever since.

A similar process led to the creation of the American Union in the late 18th century. The 13 states had emerged from the war against Britain with huge debts. They also found themselves pitched into a dangerous world, with American commerce assailed by pirates, and hostile European great powers to the north and south. Unfortunately, the constitutional arrangements inherited from the Revolutionary War were completely unsuited to dealing with the challenges. There was no real executive to speak of, Congress had no power to raise taxes to pay for a proper army or navy, and all international treaties had to be ratified by each and every one of the states before they came into force. Indeed, so loose were the bonds which held the confederation together, that many Americans feared the United States might fragment into its component parts, or even succumb to civil strife.

When the representatives of the 13 colonies came together at Philadelphia in 1787 in order to agree a constitution, they were very clear about which European union model they should follow, and which to avoid. Alexander Hamilton, later Secretary to the Treasury, and the later President James Madison, looked at the "federal system" of the "Germanic empire," and found it to be "a nerveless body, incapable of regulating its own members, insecure against external dangers, and agitated with unceasing fermentations in its own bowels."[5] In fact, of all the European precedents, the only one which found any favor among the Federalists was the Anglo-Scottish Union of 1707.[6] The constitution agreed at Philadelphia in 1787–8 showed that Americans had learned from the British and German experiences. Like the Scots and English, they determined as the preamble put it to "form a more perfect union." A strong executive was established in the shape of a presidency empowered to conduct foreign policy and conclude treaties, which were subject, however, to ratification by the two Houses of Congress. This was made up of the Senate, representing the individual states, and the House of Representatives. The rest we know: the United States eventually became the most powerful country on earth.

The historical record shows that successful unions have resulted not from gradual processes of convergence in relatively benign circumstances, but through sharp ruptures in periods of extreme crisis. They come about, not through evolution but with a "big bang." They are *events* rather than *processes*. The European political unity, which the continent so desperately needs, therefore requires a single collective act of will, by its governments and elites and ultimately by its citizens. We must follow the path set out for us more than two hundred years ago by the United Kingdom and the United States by establishing a full parliamentary, defense, and fiscal union. This is the only way of solving the debt crisis, of deterring outside predators, resolving the historical paradox of Germany's power and powerlessness in Europe, and turning Europeans and Germans into the force for good in the world that they should be.

Notes

1. I have treated these matters at much greater length in *Europe: The Struggle for Supremacy, 1453 to the Present* (London: Allen Lane, 2013) and in various articles in the *New Statesman*.

2. These figures are taken from A.J.P. Taylor, *The Struggle for Mastery in Europe, 1848–1918* (Oxford: Oxford University Press, 1954), p. xxv.

3. The connection between the European and German Questions is also made in Heinrich August Winkler, "Von der deutschen zur europäischen Frage" in *Vierteljahreshefte für Zeitgeschichte*, 63 (2015).

4. See Brendan Simms, *Three Victories and a Defeat. The Rise and Fall of the First British Empire, 1714–1783* (London: Allen Lane, 2007), pp. 51–3.

5. *The Federalist* no. 19, 8.12.1787, in Alexander Hamilton, James Madison, and John Jay, *The Federalist*, ed. J.R. Pole (Indianapolis: Hackett, 2005), pp. 99–102. For the impact of the Polish partition on the constitutional convention see Frederick W. Marks III, *Independence on Trial. Foreign Affairs and the Making of the Constitution* (Baton Rouge: Louisiana State University Press, 1973), pp. 3–51.

6. *The Federalist* no. 5, 10.11.1787, in Hamilton et al., pp. 17–18.

CHAPTER 5

DIPLOMACY AND POWER: ON THE DEPLOYMENT OF MILITARY RESOURCES IN INTERNATIONAL POLITICS

AMBASSADOR WOLFGANG ISCHINGER

Until quite recently the concept of military power was still associated with the fear of strength and the fear of invasion. Today, fear of strength has not completely disappeared in international relations—it continues to exist now as before—however alongside it we now see fear of weakness. Today, "failed" or "failing states" such as Iraq and Syria represent a danger that is as great for international security and stability as the feared Cold

War scenario of a classic invasion by an army of tanks, for example.

Twenty-five years ago, at the end of the Cold War, during the period of German reunification, the feeling arose within important sections of the American establishment that one could change the world using military power, and reconfigure it as one wished. At that time an American intellectual, Charles Krauthammer, wrote an article titled "The Unipolar Moment." In it he described a situation in which the USA could actually do anything with this overwhelming military dominance. Today we know that was a fallacy. And even in Washington today the omnipotence of the military is seen in a more skeptical light. People have understood—a realization that can be traced back to Clausewitz—that as a general rule only military problems can be solved by military force. But if a political problem must be solved, what is needed most of all is a political concept whose implementation might possibly require military involvement.

After the end of World War II the deployment of military power was thought of above all in the context of conflicts between states or groups of states. This was what European history produced all the time, and what took place constantly outside of Europe as well. Today conflict between states has certainly not disappeared from the face of the earth, but increasingly it is being replaced by—usually irregular—conflicts within states. The military conflict of today is above all a conflict within a state's borders, as illustrated by the ongoing civil war in Syria, for example. By contrast classic wars between two states have become rare. According to a study of 249 armed conflicts between 1945 and 2014, 176 of them, that is the overwhelming number of conflicts, are disputes within state borders that play out asymmetrically, that is with an important role taken by non-state operators, and in the form of civil wars.[1]

The power of these non-state actors—resistance groups, terrorist networks, and criminal organizations—has changed massively. Previously, terrorists, rebels, and insurgents hardly ever had access to military power, and, compared to the effectiveness of a state-led military power equipped with guns, tanks, or aircraft, their effectiveness was marginal. However, modern technology has changed this. Today terrorist organizations are a match for the world's strongest military powers in an asymmetrical way. This is illustrated forcefully not least by Islamic State, whose advance in the Middle East could not be halted by any regional or international initiatives thus far. Here, the horrific scenario that a terrorist group might succeed in getting hold of one or several nuclear warheads, or even build a "dirty bomb," and thus contaminate a modern industrial landscape with nuclear material, seems less and less unrealistic. The danger this presents means that the power imbalance between the omnipotent state with its military equipment and the rebel group reduces further and further.

However continual transformation is taking place not only within these actors but also in the fields of engagement in which power is exercised. If we once measured military power in the amount of guns, aircraft, ships, and military hardware, today we are starting to express military power also in whether we are able to introduce malware into the infrastructure of a potential enemy and paralyze them as a result. Just a few years ago, the idea of shutting down New York's power grids using a virus was a scenario that sounded like the stuff of science fiction. Today it can become reality. Nowadays terrorist hackers are able to attack so-called "critical infrastructures" by means of cyber-attacks, causing massive damage with a minimal amount of effort and resources. This, too, reflects the asymmetry between non-state and state actors, between resources and effects. Thus cyber-space has become a new battleground, and cyber-attacks have now become a permanent component of modern warfare. And it seems all the more threatening that in this playing field the rules of the game are still unknown.

Thus, military power is no longer measured merely in terms of military hardware, but also in the degree of availability of malware, which can be used to influence, degrade, or perhaps even destroy an enemy. This leads to what military experts call fourth-generation warfare. In the first generation, the Thirty Years' War, classic armies confronted each other. The second generation was characterized by massive firepower, as demonstrated during World War I in particular. In World War II, General Guderian's highly mobile tank units represented the third generation of warfare. In fourth-generation warfare the boundaries between conflict and peace, between soldiers and civilians, and between battlefield and protection zone are increasingly blurred. These trends recur in the tactics of hybrid warfare as well.

As a result of our history and our constitution, we in Germany believe that security outside and inside Germany are two very different things. We make a distinction between the ministry for external security, the Defense Ministry, and the ministry for internal security, the Interior Ministry. Other states operate in similar fashion. But more and more the question arises of whether this separation is still appropriate to our age, when the boundaries between civilian and military are increasingly blurred and soon the classic military battlefield may no longer be visible at all. While we waged war "over the horizon" 10 or 15 years ago, and the attackers could no longer be seen by those being attacked as a result of modern technologies, the battlefield of the future appears to be cyberspace.

The context and deployment of military power has thus undergone a comprehensive transformation over the last few decades. But how and to what ends will military power be used in international relations today?

In diplomacy, military power must always be considered the ultimate, but not the last, resource. The ultimate resource is not necessarily the resource that is employed last temporally speaking. It might well be that in a crisis an early threat or even the early deployment of military power is necessary, advisable, and crucial. The experiences gained in the politics of appeasement have shown that strategic patience cannot always curb the ambitions of aspiring major powers: if one waits too long, in certain circumstances this can be too late. Once again Syria provides a good example of this.

Traditionally, military power is a means for war or a means for victory. War means winning or losing.

War between states usually led to the capitulation of one side and the victory of the other. Today, however, war between states is no longer the dominant danger, and equally no longer the dominant way of deploying military power. Thus military power changes from a means for war into a means for strengthening security in the wider sense. In this way military power can be defined as a kind of insurance. Today the Federal Republic of Germany can say that it is completely surrounded by friendly states. The danger of an immediate threat to Germany's border has thus become negligible. Nevertheless future risks cannot be excluded completely. The Federal Republic insures itself against these risks by spending around 30 to 40 billion euros every year on the armed forces, and at the same time by belonging to the NATO alliance, thus seeking nuclear reassurance through America. In parallel, Germany is also trying to maintain this insurance cover through the European Union by means of a security policy component. Here military power serves as an insurance policy against risks that are difficult to quantify and assess—even if they have unfortunately become more tangible once again as a result of Russia's policy in Ukraine.

However, military power is not only reassurance, it is also a structural component in international relations, and not just as a way of maintaining the balance between states. In today's world our expectations, our risk assessment, our risk analyses, and our chance evaluation are also very strongly defined through military assessment. For example, the threat of military sanctions, and the concern about deploying military power in international relations leads to the structuring of expectations—at least in normal circumstances. As a result, military power as a structural component of international relations becomes a component of stability. It is to political order almost as oxygen is to breathing. We do not notice the oxygen we need to breathe; we take it as a given. It only becomes of interest when it gets scarce. The moment that air is cut off, it becomes a crucial factor. It is exactly the same with military power: if it exists, it ensures a certain amount of peace. But if it does not exist, things become very interesting very quickly.

Even in the 21st century we will have to continue to live with military power and military conflicts, even if wars between states will become increasingly less likely. Despite all attempts to contain military power and its use through international regulations and institutions—for example, the prohibition of wars of aggression in Article II no. 4 of the Charter of the United Nations—military power will remain at the heart of global power play. For this reason we cannot and must not say let's get rid of NATO and the military. President Obama was right when he said in his 2009 Nobel Prize speech: "We must begin by acknowledging the hard truth. We will not eradicate violent conflict in our lifetimes." We will not experience the absence of military conflict as a phenomenon of the modern world anytime soon.

Military power can also be a means of conflict prevention or of ending a conflict that is sometimes necessary, as demonstrated by the wars in Bosnia and Libya, and the example of Syria at the moment.

In summer 1995 European politics suffered its worst defeat of the post-war era, when almost half a million people lost their lives in Bosnia without Europe being in a position to intervene in a timely manner. It was a devastating, dramatic defeat. The goal of the negotiations that we tried to get off the ground at that time was to secure the agreement of the warring parties to a formula that had already been under discussion for many years: that in future 51% of Bosnian territory should belong to the Bosnian Muslims and 49% to the Bosnian Serbs. In fact, however, in spring 1995 the Bosnian Serbs occupied over 55% of the territory, which meant that they had no incentive to come to the negotiating table, as they would have had to give up important territory. With US support, the Croatian armed forces of the time implemented Operation Summer Storm, and in doing so decreased so much of the territory occupied by the Bosnian Serbs that, according to US radar satellite photography, the targeted proportion of 51:49 was more or less achieved. On advice from Washington, the Croatian armed forces ended their operation once this proportion had been achieved. This created the conditions under which Milošević, Tuđman, and others put their signatures to the famous Dayton Agreement three months later in Dayton, Ohio. Without this military deployment, it would not have been possible to create the conditions necessary for a peace treaty. Instead, the civil war might possibly have raged for years, with another hundred thousand dead. On the basis of these experiences we should not categorically rule out the deployment of military power.

Equally, the example of Libya has shown that the use of military power can be necessary. At the same time, the debate about international military deployment also illustrated that very differing opinions still exist between those who advocate the international "responsibility to protect" and those who fundamentally reject any intervention into the internal affairs of other countries. The "responsibility to protect" is a new form of political thinking under international law, and it is still a tender young plant, although it was resolved by an overwhelming majority in the UN General Assembly. The notion of international responsibility to protect should be mandatory in cases where a country can no longer protect its own citizens, either from foreign invasion, from terrorism, or from the wrongdoing of its own dictator. But what might be the criteria for coming to a rational judgment on the grounds for or against intervention?

For every use of military power, for every intervention, there should first exist a legal and political justification in the form of a mandate, usually through the UN Security Council. However, in the case of Kosovo, Germany's participation in the deployment of military power without the existence of a precise mandate of authorization from the Security Council, has shown that this is not an absolute requirement.

In addition a clear aim must be defined, and there must be clarity on whether this political and military aim is also achievable via the available resources. The relationship between aims and means must be correct. It cannot be permissible to deploy military power in order to exercise the responsibility to protect, only then to flop militarily leading to more and not fewer victims among the civil population. In this context the case of Libya can serve as a warning. With a mandate restricting the use of military power to air operations, it is also questionable whether the aim of protecting civilians could be achieved at all. In the case of Libya the relationship between aims and means is thus extremely hard to judge. We can still see the consequences on the ground today, and must learn from this that much more precise planning is necessary in all future cases: one should only take action if one knows that the aim is also achievable.

Conversely this also means that the necessary means must not only be readily available, but can also be deployed effectively. However this is a major problem for Europe in particular. It is scandalous how little effectiveness we in Europe achieve in relation to the resources we deploy. The states of the EU, taken together, can call on around 1.5 million soldiers, which corresponds to the number of US soldiers. At the same time the EU countries have available over six times as many different weapon systems as the US. Unfortunately, the actual military effectiveness of the EU only makes up a small fragment of US effectiveness. The deployment of European resources could hardly be more ineffective. This fragmentation is irresponsible both with regard to finances and to capabilities. The air operations in Libya have clearly shown how quickly even major EU members lose momentum. Here cooperation and integration are the only way to overcome the problem of Europe's ineffective and inefficient deployment of resources.

Ultimately the support of countries in the region in question is crucial for the success of international interventions in crises and conflicts. For example this was the case in Libya in 2011 when the Arab League itself urged the UN Security Council to intervene. In the current conflict in Syria, however, this looks very different, in light of which the countries in the region are largely following their own agendas and are thus partly even thwarting the West's offensive. But while opinions differ on the role of President Assad in any future Syria, Islamic State represents a common enemy. It is thus all the more important to bring all interested parties to the table to work out a common strategy to fight the terrorist militia, as well as a long-term solution to the conflict in Syria.

We must know whom we are siding with and whom we are against. Thus far with regard to the power relations in Syria—apart from Islamic State—we are at odds over whom we support and who should be fought. While the West, led by the US, mainly supports moderate rebel groups, and is, alongside Saudi Arabia and other Gulf States, demanding the resignation of

President Assad, Iran in particular but Russia as well are backing President Assad and support the current regime in its fight not only against Islamic State but also against these very same moderate rebel groups. Only a common regional and international strategy that clearly determines the important steps and operators in a Syrian transition process can succeed.

The case of both Libya and Syria shows that considerable skepticism towards military interventions is justified and the deployment of military power requires complex considerations. At the same time, in Syria itself it is becoming clear that political options alone are often not enough. Years ago, neither Obama nor Cameron wanted to intervene in Syria—despite previously drawn red lines. Paris did not want to act alone, and could not, and Berlin was relieved that the chalice of German military participation had passed by. But not acting also has consequences, as is now becoming clear, and looking the other way does not absolve us from responsibility. A few thousand dead have today become over 300,000—and millions of refugees. Those in Germany who were opposed to intervention warned at the time of a conflagration. In this case, the conflagration was already underway—not as a result of intervention, but as a result of collective inaction.

Thus a culture of restraint can turn into a culture of immorality.

Military power will continue to be with us. Even in the future, time and again conflicts will be dealt with using military power. We must make sure that the deployment of our military power serves clear aims, and is carried out with wide regional and international support, or rather a legitimizing mandate from the United Nations.

Note

1. Cf. Wolfgang Schreiber, "Innerstaatliche Kriege seit 1945", http://www.bpb.de/internationales/weltweit/innerstaatliche-konflikte/54508/innerstaatliche-kriege-seit-1945.

CHAPTER 6

WHO OWNS THE EURO? THE SINGLE CURRENCY AND NATIONAL POWERLESSNESS IN THE EUROPEAN DEBT CRISIS

ALBRECHT RITSCHL

Who owns the Euro? Who is the sovereign in Euroland? Is the Euro out of control? How did the Euro originate and where is it headed? Does anyone hold power over this unique and rather artificial currency? Will the Euro break up sooner or later, as no one has the power to hold it together? Conversely, will we ever get rid of the Euro when no one has the power to break it up again? This essay aims to examine some of these questions. Rather than being able to give definitive answers, it attempts to provide a few hypotheses, a limited but useful historical analogy, and avenues for further research.

The observation to start with is that the Euro in its current state is no longer what was agreed on originally. The nature of the Eurosystem has changed fundamentally since its inception. With it, the nature of the major players has changed as well; the institutions that are essential for the Euro have undergone a major process of transformation. Evidently the financial crisis since 2007 has been pivotal in this process. This chapter will argue that this transformation was the consequence of a lack of contingency clauses in the design of the Eurosystem, making it necessary to improvise to deal with the major systemic shocks emanating from the financial crisis since 2007.

The following is also an attempt to conceptualize the changes in the Euro since 2007. These changes seem to be persistent, as there are currently no signs of a return to the original constitution of the Eurosystem. Indeed, we see the first outlines of a new Euro constitution emerging in front of our eyes. Whether it is likely to endure we can only speculate, but with some likelihood the changes will be permanent.

To frame the question and keep economic technicalities to a minimum, let me examine historical models for and analogies with the Eurosystem. Any such analogy remains imperfect. Indeed the Euro is a historically unique project as it combines a centralized monetary authority with the near-absence of centralized sovereignty: the Euro is a currency without a state. The most useful comparison perhaps is therefore with the classic gold standard. The characteristic of this system was to link the value of national currencies to gold as a common standard. To be admitted into and remain within this system, countries had to adjust their monetary policy to the fluctuations in the value of gold. In practice, this implied a more or less permanent policy of fiscal austerity. For a country to remain a valued member of this system, its public debt could not grow faster than its tax revenues for extended periods, or the country's membership of the gold standard would be jeopardized. This key characteristic of the gold standard is also a key difference with regard to the Eurosystem. As a disciplinary measure, the gold standard invoked the elimination of the weakest, less so through political fiat but simply through financial markets. Indeed this threat of exit was a prerequisite for its operation. Today's "Grexit"—part encouraged, part feared—would have been considered normal under the gold standard, a crisis that would have been seen to contribute to the stabilization of the system as a whole. Historical examples from the late 19th century abound—Portugal, Spain, Italy, and Greece included.

In practice the gold standard was not simply a self-stabilizing mechanism, but was instead coordinated by the Bank of England, the central bank of the British Empire with its worldwide dominion.[1] The Bank's leading role was universally taken for granted. Until World War I, not even all member countries of the gold standard had their own central bank. The United States is the conspicuous case in point: the Federal Reserve was only created in 1914.[2] To the historian this is interesting, as America provides an example of how a highly developed economy can function without its own national monetary policy.[3] At the same time it is a pity, as the 19th-century US dollar was the early monetary union of a confederation of states that was initially only loosely knit together and lacked centralized fiscal policy. But without having had its own monetary policy, the early US must be excluded from our discussion of historical analogies to the Euro.[4]

The managed gold standard of the 19th century was a rather peculiar, living system. Even before it had spread internationally, it had become clear that in its mechanistic form conceived by early theorists, the gold standard was only a fair-weather friend to politicians and the public, unsuited to withstanding any major crises. Whenever serious shocks impacted the system, financial panics in the London market would strain the reserves of the Bank of England. More out of necessity than political doctrine, in times of crisis it resorted to suspending the redemption of banknotes or banks' other collateral in gold. Thus, when a crisis occurred, transition was made to a fiat currency almost on the fly. Once such emergencies were over, however, the Bank of England returned to its practice of redeeming banknotes in gold and to maintaining parity. Thus major wars and crises developed into contingencies in which it was deemed permissible to deviate from normal practice. What was a transgression of monetary policy in normal times was acceptable in times of crisis, so long as the reasons weighed heavily enough. This regular practice has been researched in detail in the case of 18th-century England.[5] After 1717 England had gone from its earlier bimetallic mixed system to a purely gold-based currency. Under Isaac Newton, in his second job as Warden and Master of the Royal Mint, gold had been deliberately overvalued in relation to silver. Thus the public could pay their debts and taxes in the now relatively cheaper gold coins instead of in silver coins, which were undervalued compared to their metallic market value. Gresham's Law whereby bad money drives out good came into effect: the silver coinage disappeared from circulation and England acquired its gold standard. This system proved to be extremely robust. Previously, the most common method of financing wars and major contingencies had been to debase the coinage and manipulate the exchange rate between silver and gold. From now on, in the event of war, England simply suspended gold transactions at the Mint. This was made easier by the fact that already during the Glorious Revolution of 1688, the Royal budget had been strictly separated from that of Parliament, and the army had *e facto* become a parliamentary army.[6] As a result, England's wars in the 18th century could be financed rather easily by borrowing, and the public put up with the temporary suspension of gold convertibility without complaint. Confidence was based on the expectation that, after the war ended, the gold cover would be restored at the previous parity and bondholders would be paid off in full value. Thus the gold standard operated normally during peacetime, and in an exceptional way in times of war and states of emergency. The master and guardian of these exceptional contingencies was the Bank of England, which gave the Bank a great deal of authority even during peacetime. This authority was based on the public's trust in a return to a normal monetary situation once the contingency was over. Institutionally this consensus was underpinned by trust in Parliament, whose House of Commons was itself largely an assembly of merchants that owned much of the public debt. This arrangement gained traction through the frequent interplay of exceptional contingencies and a successful return to normal, however painful the adjustment and austerity were. Institutional safeguards combined with the establishment of a good reputation over the course of several crises to create a climate in which the risk of currency debasement was considered minimal. The success of the system lay in not giving in to what is called the time consistency problem of monetary policy while at the same time having a flexible rule that dealt with major crisis. That is, it credibly committed itself against the temptation to permanently debase the coinage and thus dispossess the holders of currency and public bonds. At the same time, it was flexible enough not to have to stick to the rigid rules of gold-backing during major crises, with the harmful effects on the economy that such austerity during a crisis would entail. In other words, one could dilute the currency for a while if necessary, but was credibly committed to stabilizing and restoring the old parity, without a loss in value, as soon as the contingency was over. This ingenious system has been termed a contingent commitment technology. To make it work, however, required coordination between the Bank of England and Parliament, or, in modern-day terms, between monetary and fiscal policies.[7]

All of England's major wars in the 18th century, including in part the wars against revolutionary France, were financed in this way, without having to resort to drastic tax increases. In times of war, Britain could fall back on a highly elastic capital market that made financial resources available without much problem. In all cases the subsequent return to the gold standard successfully re-established the old parity, albeit with serious economic crisis symptoms, but without a crisis of confidence in the financial system itself.

The most painful instance of such an adjustment only came after the Napoleonic Wars, when England's sovereign debt as a result of the war had spiraled to about 300% of GDP. By comparison, Greece's national debt to GDP ratio during the recent debt crisis has been around 170%. By way of further comparison, the London ultimatum of 1921 fixed Germany's repa-rations after World War I at 260% of Germany's 1913 GDP (the Allies were really serious about the payment of around 100%).[8] Of course, Great Britain was undisputedly the leading economic and military world power of the 19th century. To service Britain's debts after the Napoleonic Wars, a tough policy of austerity was introduced; the national budget after servicing the debt remained balanced for decades. In so doing, it created primary surpluses to pay interest on the accumulated debts. The social consequences of this drastic policy did not go unnoticed, and are described, for example, by Charles Dickens, or by Friedrich Engels in his study of the condition of the working class in England.[9] Over the course of almost a century, this policy of sustained austerity gradually reduced England's national debt to GDP ratio, until it ultimately reached 30% shortly before World War I: from 300% to 30%! This is one of the few instances when fiscal austerity actually worked. To be sure, the level of debt itself did not fall. The decline in the ratio was entirely due to the steady increase in GDP and, along with it, in tax revenue.[10]

Institutionally the creation of the Euro took a rather different course. Instead of linking the currency to gold and thereby relinquishing or centralizing control over the value of money in the hands of the central bank of a leading country, a supranational institution was created. Not tasking an existing player such as Germany's Bundesbank was a decision with far-reaching consequences, as we know today.[11] In regard to these two aspects, the Eurosystem is weaker than the classic gold standard. On the other hand, national currencies in the Eurosystem were abolished completely. Instead, the Euro was established as sole legal tender in all Member States, and no provision was made for a Member State to exit the monetary union. To this extent the Euro is both weaker and stronger than the gold standard. It is weaker to the extent that it is a purely fiat currency, and the institutional precautions to defend its monetary value are not particularly strong. However, it is also considerably stronger to the extent that there are substantial barriers to exit for individual Member States. Leaving the Euro is not so easy, no matter how spectacularly Greece's outgoing Finance Minister Varoufakis zoomed off on his motorbike after handing in his resignation. Likewise, it is also not easy to expel a Member State, as German Finance Minister Wolfgang Schäuble discovered to his dismay in 2015. The Eurosystem's cohesive forces are rather powerful, and were apparently underestimated by all concerned.

When the Eurosystem was first created, no consideration was given to such things. The first Euro regime at its inception was characterized by concerns about its obvious weakness at the time. This was the threatening loss of anti-inflationary credibility during the transition of power from Germany's Bundesbank as the center of the old system to the European Central

Bank as guardian of the new Euro currency. As under a fiat currency no automatic stabilizer for the value of money can exist, the creators of the Euro system tried their hand at a set of fiscal policy rules, the convergence criteria of the Maastricht Treaty. Only those countries that met the debt criterion of 60% and the deficit criterion of 3% of GDP should be accepted into this elite club. It was hoped to create a debt-policy straitjacket of good fiscal conduct to make the participants lean and fit for the Eurozone. It could hardly have been any other way. If no one can be excluded, and even the markets cannot bowl out anyone who has misbehaved, then the weakest in the system can always band together to dispose of their debts through inflation, at the cost of the stronger Members who have maintained sound national budgets. The nightmare of the Maastricht architects was not sovereign bankruptcy and debt crisis, but a future takeover of power by inflation friends in the ECB whose aim would be to transform the nascent Euro into a weak, inflationary currency. This is what the Maastricht criteria were invented to counteract.

In its original form we could explicitly call this currency system the "Waigel Euro," after Germany's finance minister during the 1990s whose policy was to create a Eurosystem of the fiscally sound. Compliance with Waigel's fiscal criteria was never perfect. Germany itself numbered among the first to violate the Maastricht criteria in 2005. In a serious blow to the credibility of the system, it was condoned although its violation of the rules was unquestionable. Overall, however, the Waigel Euro did fulfill its purpose during the early years. Counter to the predictions of many a doomsayer, the inflation rate remained low, and the Member States' national debts did not rise excessively. With a little goodwill as well as a nod and a wink, it would be fair to say that until the 2007 financial crisis hit, the Waigel Euro was a success and its opponents had been proved wrong.

This was not sheer coincidence. The Maastricht criteria that are much maligned today were based on the resilience of tax systems in the face of medium-sized economic fluctuations. Perhaps more than half the countries that had joined the Eurozone had not met at least one, and in some cases neither of the convergence criteria. In the absence of a more serious crisis, however, the weaknesses of the system were not exposed. This only changed with the advent of the international finan- cial crisis of 2007, for which no institutional provisions had been made in the design of the Eurosystem. It was this crisis which killed off the Maastricht criteria very quickly. Just like the ideal form of the gold standard, the

Waigel Euro was only a fair-weather friend, proving to be useless in the heavy weather since 2008. And yet the Euro is still with us today.

The reason is that our monetary system today is not what it was until 2007. Under the pressures of the crisis, a back-up constitution for the Eurosystem has taken shape, not in principle dissimilar to that of the gold standard. Whether the nature of the Eurosystem has changed irreversibly as a result, or whether a return to normal is still possible as in the days of the old Bank of England, is debatable and yet difficult to predict.[12]

These changes to the constitution of the Eurosystem took place over several phases. The first was the intervention of the core European countries led by Germany in the first Greek debt crisis of May 2010, where a twin strategy was pursued. On the one hand, Greece's debts were guaranteed under the so-called European Stability Mechanism (ESM). In non-technical terms, this was Greece's bailout. On the other hand, the bailout conditions committed Greece to a severe austerity policy. The monetary system created as a result can be termed the "Schäuble Euro," after Germany's finance minister who decided underwriting Greece's debts was preferable to risking a return of the international banking crisis. This intervention in the Greek debt crisis could gain credibility because Greece is small by comparison with the entire Eurozone, and taking on its debt service was, after all, not an unsustainable burden.

The Eurosystem nevertheless changed fundamentally as a result of this intervention. Under the gold standard, disciplining debtor nations automatically followed the rules of the market: the loss of credibility would lead to a meltdown of their gold and foreign exchange reserves, and at the end there was either a harsh restructuring program for its public finances, or an exit of the country in question from the system. Under the Waigel Euro no guidance or rule for such a contingency had been provided for. At best one could conclude from the convergence criteria and from the however ambiguous non-liability clause of Art. 104b of the Treaty on the European Union that in the event of a debt crisis a Member State of the Euro would have to manage on its own. So long as this was not tested in practice, the idea of the Waigel Euro as an elite club like the gold standard could live on.

The legal debate about whether the Maastricht Treaty flatly ruled out bailouts or just excluded mutual liability does not matter very much here. Economically speaking, any commitment against bailouts between Member States had to lose its credibility as soon as the debt crisis of one Member State became systemically important and threatened to shake up the financial position of the creditor countries as well. This "too big to fail" problem is well known from corporate finance and has been documented in numerous examples of rescuing ailing large companies. The bank bailouts in all leading economic countries at the peak of the international financial crisis in fall 2008 again provided abundant evidence. For the Eurosystem, however, any such rescue operation meant the beginning of a systemic change. During this process, two conspicuous features came to light. On the one hand, the threat to expel a failing debtor country was and remained ineffective. Unlike the gold standard, from now on the Eurosystem was no longer an elite club. On the other hand, the bailout entailed a hitherto unknown loss of fiscal sovereignty on the part of the debtor country concerned. The Waigel Euro had been fiercely criticized for having a common monetary policy but not a common fiscal policy. Under pressure of the Greek debt crisis, this changed and the criticism lost force. The deflationary pressure that was inherent in the market operation of the gold standard now became the objective of political action, a result of centrally led fiscal policy after 2010. The body managing this policy was the German Finance Ministry, and the Waigel Euro turned into a Schäuble Euro.

There is a valid intellectual case to be made in defense of the Schäuble Euro, the new system based on bailout-cum-austerity rather than an expulsion from the club of the best. Had the international crisis been over by, say, 2012, and had Greece subsequently enjoyed economic recovery, the Greek bailout would have remained a footnote of history. Hopes for a short crisis and swift international recovery would indeed rationalize the decision to bail out Greece. Then, divergence from the Maastricht criteria would have only been temporary and could have been corrected through mild doses of austerity. The rest of the task would have been accomplished by a sustainable economic recovery, whereby the burden of debt would grow more slowly than the economy, following the example of 19th-century England. Thus, while a bailout was against the Maastricht rules and could not eliminate the debt problem of Greece, it would at least postpone its solution to a hopefully more favorable moment in the future.

This first incarnation of the Schäuble Euro, with the German finance minister at the helm of a newly coordinated European fiscal policy, nevertheless had a credibility problem. For what happens if the debt crisis migrates from a country that is indeed systemically important, albeit small, to a larger country in the

Eurozone? In this case even the pockets of the German Finance Ministry would not be deep enough for a rescue operation, and the crisis would not be controllable through fiscal policy. Soon dubbed "too big to bail," this specter appeared on the horizon when in 2011 the returns on Southern European—i.e. Italian—government bonds began to climb to dangerously high levels.

Schäuble's Euro was not able to cope. Even Germany, France, and the remaining smaller net creditors north of the Alps combined would have been incapable of withstanding a speculative raid, for example, on Italy's enormous national debt.

This emergency was again resolved in a way that had not been foreseen in the original constitution of the Euro, and which strictly speaking ran counter to it. This solution was the announcement of the ECB's open market policy under the Outright Monetary Transactions (OMT) Program. An open-market policy means that the central bank intervenes in the secondary market for sovereign bonds. If the yields on Southern European sovereign bonds kept on rising, the ECB would carry out bond price support transactions through a massive purchase of sovereign bonds, and thus depress the returns on these bonds almost arbitrarily. At the time of its announcement in 2012 the OMT program was simply a declaration of intent, and was only implemented much later. The mere announcement made the risk premiums on Southern European bonds collapse like a pricked bubble. However, in this program the ECB was operating on the very edge of an infringement of its constitution, which drew fierce criticism in German media and brought about a lawsuit in Germany's Federal Constitutional Court. The question was whether the ECB was carrying out an illegal program of state financing. According to the Maastricht regulations, the purchase of sovereign bonds by the ECB was tightly limited, for the same reasons that lay behind the convergence criteria on national debt and deficit. If, under normal circumstances, a central bank buys large quantities of sovereign bonds and treasury bills, the national budget will be financed by the printing press to an ever-increasing extent. Two major German currency reforms in the 20th century provide eloquent proof of the ramifications of such a policy. It was therefore controversial as to whether or not there was a case here of state financing through monetary policy, an illegal combination of fiscal and monetary policy. In the end the constitutional judges held back from cutting the ECB off short by legal means—the OMT program was not outlawed.

This course of events had far-reaching implications. Using an instrument that was not part of its original toolkit, and whose legitimacy is still questioned today in Germany, the ECB was suddenly able to assume the role of master of the emergency. What under normal circumstances would be strictly prohibited becomes admissible under the stress of the crisis as an urgent, simply irrefutable guiding principle that even the German Constitutional Court did not dare to oppose.

The parallel with the classic gold standard is striking. In a crisis the margin requirements for the currency are temporarily suspended, and state financing by the printing press or at least substantial open market purchases becomes permissible. Just as in the olden days the obligation to redeem banknotes in gold was suspended in emergency situations, now the prohibition on buying government bonds was suspended. Not unlike in the past, there arose almost overnight an informal monetary back-up constitution that had not been envisaged before, and which ran diametrically counter to the spirit of the monetary constitution under normal circumstances.

Carl Schmitt, a prominent constitutional expert of the Weimar Republic who would later become notorious for his flirtation with the Nazis, once remarked that he who decides on proclaiming the state of emergency is the true sovereign.[13] At the time, the sovereignty issue in question in Germany was the president's power to issue emergency decrees under Art. 48 of the Weimar Constitution. Schmitt saw the state of emergency as a case of extreme danger that cannot be defined in advance by the legal system and the constitution. According to Schmitt the only measure of an institution's sovereignty is its power over the state of emergency, and a constitution can best be interpreted by analyzing who has the powers to act in this situation. Modern constitutions, Schmitt argued, have the tendency to completely eliminate a sovereign in this sense. But he doubted whether any constitution could also eliminate the exceptional contingency that underlies the state of emergency. That, to Schmitt, was not a legal question or one that any constitutional design could predetermine.

During the classic gold standard the Bank of England was the master of the state of emergency, and without any doubt the true sovereign of the monetary constitution. By contrast, in the state of emergency of the Eurosystem, there were two rival centers of power who were wrestling openly in conflict with each other for the power to act. The first of these two pretenders to the sovereign's throne was the German Finance Minister with his intervention in the first Greek crisis outside of the law. The second was the ECB under Mario Draghi with its announcement of the OMT policy, again outside of the law, when the debt crisis threatened to spread to the Southern European countries as a whole. In this second phase of the Eurozone debt crisis, the law of action transferred from the first pretender to the second. One apparent reason is that the German Finance Ministry was running out of further options due to the sheer dimension of the looming threat, while the ECB arguably had unlimited scope for action. Activating the printing press, the ECB was the only institution that had the tools to effectively repel speculative attacks against the weakest Euro states, and thus to prevent the otherwise unavoidable collapse of the Eurosystem. In this way the ECB became the master of the state of emergency and hence the true sovereign of the Eurozone. The monetary system created by the ECB through the use of its emergency powers can be called the Draghi Euro. It is the product of extralegal action in an extreme contingency, exactly as Carl Schmitt described, that even the judicial guardians of the German constitution dared not prohibit, as otherwise the imminent collapse of the Eurozone would have been sealed.

However we can see that the ECB has not maintained its sovereignty over this crisis unreservedly, and once more this takes us back to Greece. When the Greek debt crisis flared up for the second time, the ECB's hands were tied. For the ECB is not in control of the market for Greek government bonds. The ECB's constitution explicitly rules out intervention on behalf of a country that has already lost access to international capital markets. Had the ECB started open-market operations with large quantities of Greek government bonds, it would certainly have entered the core area of state financing, which it was forbidden to do. Thus the ball was once again in the court of the German Finance Minister—for a moment, the Schäuble Euro was back.

This takes us back to our opening question. Let us pause for a moment and ask not which Euro we prefer, whether we like Schäuble more than Draghi, or if we reject the whole construct and would rather return to the Deutschmark. With regard to the extreme contingency that the financial crisis was and the absence of any contingency planning in the Maastricht system, the question is who is the true master of the state of emergency, who is sovereign in Euroland?

In their second attempt to tackle the Greek crisis in 2015, the finance ministers regained the initiative. For a moment the previous system was re-established, whereby sovereignty in the sense of mastery of the emergency once more lay with the German Finance

Ministry. This second edition of the Schäuble Euro is in many respects a repeat of the first, an attempt to return to the elite club, where again the emergency is dealt with by bailouts-cum-austerity. It comes as no surprise that this rerun of the Schäuble Euro was equally unable to convince the skeptics in Germany, as the credibility problems of this system remain the same. If thought through completely, the Schäuble Euro II would mean that time and again we would be rescuing a weak country such as Greece, which is possibly structurally incapable of lasting reform by means of bailouts and an austerity policy decreed from abroad. Hopes of a short duration of the Greek crisis, a quick turnaround into self-sustained recovery, and of an only short-term infringement of the Maastricht Treaty, are clearly no longer justifiable. This makes the current bailout the father of the next, followed by the next, and so on. With the bailouts to Greece, Europe has already embarked on a series of fiscal transfers, irregular and improvised as they may be. This is not a question of whether we want fiscal transfers or not, but rather merely a statement of facts: a system of fiscal equalization transfers in the Eurozone is already in existence. The only question is what we should call this child: should it be a legitimate child of the Eurozone with a gradually developing fiscal constitution, or do we want it to be the illegitimate child of a politics of contradictions and avoidance, that undertakes "haircuts" without acknowledging them as such, and that has created a transfer union without calling it by name?

The Draghi Euro gives all powers to the ECB, not because it has been formally handed the keys by its makers but because the ECB is the only institution in the position "to do whatever it takes." This system already operates outside the now narrower confines of the Greek debt problem. Paradoxically, it has become more stable because of the temporary solution of the Greek debt crisis. As a consequence of its increased gravitas, the Bank has assumed more and more competences, particularly in the area of banking supervision. Setting up banking supervision in a central bank is the devil's work, as it puts the central bank in a conflict of interests between monetary and banking policy. This has meant that an institution whose aims are arguably not the same as those of the Bundesbank, has acquired an enormous degree of authority and power. At present, no one can predict what the return to a normal constitution of the Eurozone's monetary system will look like, what time frame is necessary for this, and whether the ECB can return to a traditional monetary policy resembling the values of the

Maastricht Treaty. European monetary policy is still in the state of emergency described by Carl Schmitt, standing in for the fiscal policy that is incapable of action given its institutional limitations. This situation is not without irony, as much of the research on the political dynamics of hyperinflation has assumed a causality going from powerful but inflation-prone fiscal authorities to stability-oriented but weak central banks. In spite of the reversal of roles apparent in the Eurozone crisis, the outcome might still be the same: an extensive blurring of monetary and fiscal policy, with all the conceivable consequences and ramifications. This would be rather the opposite of the dominant position the Bank of England had over the state of emergency during the classic gold standard. In other words and simply put, whether the ECB will maintain its power in good times and bad will ultimately depend on its willpower to declare an end to the state of emergency.

Conversely we can ask whether the Schäuble Euro II with its combination of bailout and austerity politics represents a workable alternative, and what the success criteria for that would be. The basic assumption of Germany's policy during the Eurozone debt crisis has remained the avoidance of debt haircuts wherever possible. If this policy is thought through, the only remaining alternatives for the debtor nations are continued austerity policies in the hope of bringing their economic system closer to the German model, or exit—*tertium non ɩatur*, there is no third way. Without a clean fiscal solution to the Eurozone debt problem, the explosiveness of this problem would only be further exacerbated and carried to extremes if the ECB phased out its open-market policy with regard to Southern European government bonds. If debt reduction is not deemed acceptable, and if no pro-market reforms are implemented to make their economies structurally more similar to the German model, an exit of the Mediterranean countries, a "Club Med" exit, might become very difficult to avoid. In such a case we would see a return to a Deutschmark zone, perhaps this time without France. The borders of this Deutschmark zone would run through the Upper Rhine Valley, straight past Schäuble's own constituency.

To conclude, we may ask what will happen if nothing happens. It can easily be argued that the Greek debt renegotiations in 2015 resulted in a serious defeat for the concept of the Schäuble Euro. For Greece's forced departure from the Eurozone, the Grexit, did not happen. But without Grexit, and without lasting debt relief, a sustainable fiscal solution for the Greek debt problem can only be found in further financial support, and a system of fiscal transfers in one form or another. Under the current state of things, a self-sustaining Greek recovery with a balance of payments surplus is a long way off. What happens, then, if in the future neither Grexit nor debt restructuring takes place? This scenario is quite likely. The barriers to Grexit are substantial, those for an expulsion are even more so, and those for a comprehensive reorganization of sovereign debts in the Eurozone seem currently insurmountable. Without a solution to the problem of sovereign debt, however, the future of the Draghi Euro is the perpetuation of the state of emergency: a Euro that is longer-lasting than we thought, more malleable than we wanted, and in which an unregulated system of fiscal transfers is binding the weak countries to the strong, whether they want it or not. As long as the debt issue in Europe remains unresolved, one thing will remain the same: the position of the ECB as the unchallenged manager of the crisis, the master of the perpetual state of emergency, and the true if extra-constitutional sovereign of the Eurozone.

Notes

1. The standard work on this topic is: Barry Eichengreen, "Conducting the International Orchestra: Bank of England Leadership under the Classical Gold Standard, 1880–1913" in *Journal of International Money an∙ Finance* 6, 1 (1987), pp. 5–29.

2. On the history of the Fed, see Allan Meltzer, *A History of the Fe∙eral Reserve, vol. 1, 1913–1951* (Chicago: University of Chicago Press, 2002).

3. See the following studies: Ellis W. Tallman, "Gold Shocks, Liquidity, and the United States Economy During the National Banking Era" in *Explorations in Economic History* 35 (1998); Ellis W. Tallman and Jon R Moen, "Liquidity Creation without a Central Bank: Clearing House Loan Certificates in the Banking Panic of 1907" in *Journal of Financial Stability* 8, 4 (2012).

4. See however Thomas Sargent's Nobel Prize speech, "United States Then, Europe Now" in *Journal of Political Economy* 120, 1 (2012).

5. The standard work on this topic is: Michael Bordo and Eugene White, "A Tale of Two Currencies: British and French Finance During the Napoleonic Wars" in *Journal of Economic History* 51 (1991).

6. This step has for a long time been regarded by economic historians as the birth of modern economic growth in general. Cf. Douglass C. North and Robert P. Thomas, *The Rise of the Western Worl∙* (Cambridge: Cambridge University Press, 1971). A modern approach to the topic is Patrick O'Brien, "The Nature and Historical Evolution of an Exceptional Fiscal State and Its Possible Significance for the Precocious Commercialization and Industrialization of the British Economy from Cromwell to Nelson" in *Economic History Review* 64, 2 (2011).

7. The modern interpretation of the British gold standard as a contingent commitment to overcoming the time consistency problem goes back to Michael Bordo and Finn Kydland, "The Gold Standard as a Rule: An Essay in Exploration" in *Explorations in Economic History* 32 (1995).

8. For our purposes an interesting possible model for the consequences of Greece leaving the Eurozone is the connection between a debt burden that is rejected by the general public and the subsequent inflationary destruction of the monetary system. See the extensive discussion in Gerald Feldman, *The Great Disorder. Politics, Economics, and Society in the German Inflation, 1914–1924* (Oxford: Oxford University Press, 1993). See also numerical data in Albrecht Ritschl, "The German Transfer Problem, 1920–33: A Sovereign-Debt Perspective" in *European Review of History* 19, 6 (2012).

9. Charles Dickens, *Oliver Twist* (London, 1838); Friedrich Engels, *The Condition of the Working Class in England*, trans. Florence Kelley (New York, 1887; original German edition: Leipzig, 1845).

10. Albrecht Ritschl, "Sustainability of High Public Debt: What the Historical Record Shows" in *Swedish Economic Policy Review* 3 (1996).

11. See the standard work on the creation of the Euro by Harold James, *Making the European Monetary Union* (Cambridge, Mass: Harvard University Press, 2012).

12. On the history of the Euro crisis see Hans-Werner Sinn, *The Euro Trap* (Oxford: Oxford University Press, 2014).

13. Carl Schmitt, *Political Theology. Four Chapters on the Concept of Sovereignty*, trans. George Schwab (Cambridge and London: MIT Press, 1985).

CHAPTER 7

ON THE VALUE OF COMPANIES' POLITICAL CONNECTIONS

JÖRG ROCHOLL

"Merchants and master manufacturers are, in this order, the two classes of people who commonly employ the largest capitals, and who by their wealth draw to themselves the greatest share of the public consideration. [...] As their thoughts, however, are commonly exercised rather about the interest of their own particular branch of business, than about that of the society, their judgment, even when given with the greatest candour (which it has not been upon every occasion), is much more to be depended upon with regard to the former of those two objects, than with regard to the latter. [...] The proposal of any new law or regulation of commerce which comes from this order, ought always to be listened to with great precaution, and ought never to be adopted till after having been long and carefully examined, not only with the most scrupulous, but with the most suspicious attention."[1]

Questioning the value of companies' political connections has a long history. Adam Smith writes that companies have a considerable interest in influencing political decisions in their favor and in increasing their economic success by so doing. In countries with a weak legal system and a high degree of corruption, the value of such influence would be considerable, as here the possible gains are also extremely high, and the risk of those involved being discovered and convicted are extremely low. By contrast, in countries with strong legal systems, competitive advantages for companies which have political connections should not apply, or at least not to the same extent. In these countries government officials or other responsible persons would be running a great risk if they made decisions in favor of particular companies, decisions that privileged not the public but the private interest of these companies. It is thus unsurprising that the first empirical investigations into the question of the value of companies' political connections were carried out in countries with weaker legal systems. One example is a research project on Indonesian companies that were linked to the family of Indonesian President Suharto. When the President's health began to seriously decline, the share prices of the companies that were linked to him and his family fell.[2] This starting point prompted my co-authors Eitan Goldman, Jongil So, and myself to write two scientific articles investigating whether companies' political connections have a value even in the USA, a country with a strong and independent legal system and, if so, how this value can be explained. These two articles form the basis of the following discussion.

1. HOW VALUABLE ARE THE POLITICAL CONNECTIONS OF COMPANIES IN THE USA?

Companies can build up political connections in various ways, and three opportunities provide good examples. First, they can donate to political parties. This opportunity is particularly pertinent since the 2010 groundbreaking decision of the US Supreme Court in the case of Citizens United. Second, companies can appoint former politicians to their boards and rely on the latter using their political expertise and networks to the company's advantage. Third, they can try to participate in the political process through associations or other kinds of lobbying. Not all these opportunities are equally suitable for an empirical assessment of the value of political connections for companies. For example, it is proven that US companies which donate more to political parties demonstrate better share returns.[3] However, it is unclear whether there is a causal relationship in the sense that donating companies have better political access and an economically more successful operation because of this. Indeed, the opposite causal relationship could also pertain, in that successful companies simply have more financial resources at their disposal, enabling them to participate in politics. Equally, it is hard to measure the value of political connections via lobbying, as many of these activities are (deliberately) lacking in transparency and thus cannot be measured. In our study, we measured a company's political connections by whether and to what extent the board members of an individual S&P 500 company demonstrate prior activity as politicians.[4]

Alongside the definition of a company's political connection, we looked at how the value of this connection can be measured. Here once again in the question of causality it does not help to know that companies with political connections have higher enterprise values. Political connections might actually help companies be more successful, but successful companies could simply be more attractive and thus more successful in attracting politicians to work for them. For this reason in our study we used two kinds of unforeseen events, on the one hand the *ex-ante* (and as would later transpire, also *ex-post*) uncertain outcome of the US presidential election in 2000, and on the other the appointment of former politicians to the boards of US companies, in order to measure the reaction of the share prices of companies with political connections.

Our findings show a clear picture. In the days immediately after the 2000 US presidential election, which ended with the victory of the Republican candidate George W. Bush over the Democratic candidate Al Gore, the value of those companies, whose boards consisted exclusively of former Republican politicians, rose markedly, whereas the value of companies with exclusively former Democratic politicians fell. During this presidential election further results could be obtained because the election result was legally contested for several weeks, and the final result only became clear in mid-December. The Florida Supreme Court's decision on December 8, 2000 to order a re-count led to companies with Republican connections losing value, whereas companies with Democratic connections gained in value.

The opposite reaction could be seen on December 13, 2000, when Al Gore admitted defeat, and thus the final decision as to the next US president was made in favor of George W. Bush and the Republicans. These findings cannot be explained by the fact that certain industries—for example, the media and the Democrats, or the tobacco industry and the Republicans—are more strongly linked to one particular party, and thus display positive or negative reactions in their share prices independent of the party's attitude to this industry. The results remain unchanged even when such industry effects are taken into consideration.

In part two of this article we find that companies that appoint politicians to their boards can enjoy a rise in share price on the announcement of such appointments. This positive reaction is particularly pronounced when these former politicians are nominated for membership of a company's board for the first time. On the occasion of further nominations the effect is positive as before, but less pronounced, which suggests that a certain amount of wear and tear emerges, which could also be called the "teabag effect." The observation of a generally positive share price reaction to the appointment of former politicians can be seen independently of the party political background of the board members and the functional and industry relevant expertise that they have acquired as politicians. This evidence underlines the fact that political experience and expertise have a value for companies unrelated to specific political activity and such activity's relationship to the former politician's later activity within the company. This positive reaction contrasts with the reaction to the appointments of new board members who have other professional and non-political backgrounds, appointments that on average produce no change in share price. These results suggest that political connections have an effect on companies' share prices and influence their value. However, it remains unclear where this increase in value comes from.

2. DO COMPANIES' POLITICAL CONNECTIONS HAVE AN INFLUENCE IN THE AWARDING OF GOVERNMENT CONTRACTS?

In the second article, my co-authors and I turned to the question of how to explain this increase in value in the case of politically connected companies.[5] In earlier studies by other researchers it was shown, among other results, that companies with political connections have improved access to finance and have a greater chance of being bailed out by state funds if they get into difficulties. We concentrated on the question of whether and to what extent the increase in value of politically connected companies can be explained by their increased involvement in the awarding of government contracts. Government contracts represent a substantial amount and are thus highly sought after by companies. This is an example from the period between 1990 and 2004 that we used in our research. During this period, some 11.5 million government contracts were awarded, representing a total value of more than 3.1 trillion US dollars. Immediately after the terrorist attacks of September 11, 2001 and the subsequent crises in Afghanistan and Iraq, both values rose considerably once more. It is thus not surprising that those very companies which owe a large proportion of their turnover to government contracts frequently have former politicians, both Democratic and Republican, on their boards.

Just as in the first part of the study, two challenges emerged during empirical assessment. First, the question arose of how companies' political connections can be identified. We tackled this challenge as before and again measured whether and to what extent companies had former politicians on their boards. Second, the process of awarding government contracts does not take place in public, and it can in principle be influenced by both the legislature and the executive. Thus in our study we looked at both the 1994 congressional elections and the 2000 presidential elections that led to a change in power in both the executive and the legislature.

Once again our results showed a clear picture. The 1994 congressional elections that led to a Republican win and a change of power in Congress meant that companies with Republican links received considerably more government contracts in the four-year period after the elections than in the previous four-year period, while exactly the opposite effect could be seen in the case of companies with Democratic connections. A similar picture emerges when comparing the four-year period before and after the 2000 presidential elections that led to a transfer of power in the executive from the Democrats to the Republicans. Once again, companies with Republican links won considerably more contracts after the election than before, whereas companies with Democratic connections lost contracts. These results indicate that companies' political connections have a significant influence on the awarding of government contracts to these companies. Thus the awarding of government contracts constitutes a further, substantial opportunity for companies with a political connection to the governing party to profit from this connection—and thus explains the rise in their share prices after the 2000 US presidential elections.

3. SUMMARY AND CONCLUSION

The two scientific articles we have described address the central question of how companies and politics are linked, and whether companies' political connections have an effect on their value. The first article shows that US S&P 500 companies with former politicians on their boards achieve positive share returns when the party with which their board members are associated is successfully elected. At the same time, the share prices of US companies profit from appointing these former politicians to their boards. The second article shows that companies' political links have a significant effect on the extent to which these companies win government contracts. Overall, the evidence shows that the political connections of companies in the US increase the value of these companies.

This leads to the important question of the classification of these results, as they can be interpreted in very different ways. One positive interpretation might be that during their political lives politicians acquire such considerable expertise and develop such a valuable network that they represent a particularly significant asset for those companies that can appoint executives with these qualities. Following this interpretation their use in lobbying could help create a better information base for political decision-makers and thus bring about better decisions overall. A less positive interpretation that can be drawn from the aforementioned example of Indonesia, but also from many others, would be that politicians have a particular ability to understand the opaque circles of power in all their murkiest depths; in this case the appearance of corruption is not far away. The dividing line between these two interpretations, that is, between legitimate lobbying and reprehensible corruption, is very fine, and thus it is particularly important to describe the criteria that can ensure that companies' political connections are employed in a transparent and accountable way.

First of all this involves companies' duty to uphold the standards of proper corporate governance, that is, the generally acknowledged principles of good business practice, and the creation of complete transparency when it comes to political connections of whatever kind. Linked to this is the creation and maintenance of a particular political culture with institutionalized checks and balances: for example, a critical public sphere including an independent and strong media, organizations such as the Federal Audit Office or NGOs such as Transparency International, strong parliaments with appropriate committees of inquiry, and other monitoring mechanisms.

Notes

1. Adam Smith, *An Inquiry into the Nature and Causes of the Wealth of Nations* (London, 1793), vol. I, p. 396.

2. Raymond Fisman, "Estimating the Value of Political Connections" in *American Economic Review* 91, 4 (September 2001), pp. 1095–1102.

3. Michael J. Cooper, Huseyin Gulen, and Alexei V. Ovtchinnikov, "Corporate Political Contributions and Stock Returns" in *Journal of Finance* 65, 2, (2010), pp. 687–724.

4. Eitan Goldman, Jörg Rocholl, and Jongil So, "Do Politically Connected Boards Affect Firm Value?" in *Review of Financial Studies* 22, 6, (2009), pp. 2331–360.

5. Eitan Goldman, Jörg Rocholl, and Jongil So, "Politically Connected Boards of Directors and the Allocation of Procurement Contracts" in *Review of Finance* 17, 5, (2013), pp. 1617–648.

CHAPTER 8

THE POWER OF DATA AND
DATA QUALITY

THOMAS HOEREN

Power has a lot to do with knowledge, access to, and utilization of data. But in the context of the debate about power, the question of data quality is hardly ever raised. This is because legal standards for data quality are lacking. The first attempts to regulate this question can be found hidden in Art. 6 of the EU Data Protection Directive and in the regulation on scoring in Section 28b of the German Federal Data Protection Act (BDSG). From this, with the help of initial research attempts by computer science and sociology, we can develop a provisional, fragmentary framework for legal standards in data quality, as I will demonstrate in the following ten theses.

1. THE SILENCE OF THE LAMBS: WHY DOES RESEARCH HAVE NOTHING TO SAY ABOUT DATA QUALITY?

Data are the backbone of power. Only someone who knows something and has access to data can control, plan, and effect changes. Data are often interpreted as the currency of the digital economy, not without reason. So it is all the more astonishing that until now there has been hardly any debate about the protection of data quality within the discussion of power and powerlessness.[1] What remains of the power of an organization such as Google when spectacular big data cases such as their Google Flu Trends turned out to be *ex-post* false?[2]

This ignorance is still promoted by articles in the daily press that extol the sloppiness of data research as an actual asset in big data, for example, as here in the *Süddeutsche Zeitung*:

Large amounts of data, dirty data, results that indicate a trend but do not provide an exact result—in
just about all of this the big data method contradicts
the way in which statisticians have worked up to
now. But if large amounts of data are processed it is
this sheer mass whose analysis ultimately brings one
very close to one's goal.[3]

This denies the fact that for jurists the question of
data quality arises and must arise in at least three situations. The first is the question of buying raw data:
for the buyer the issue is essentially the protection of
the contractually stipulated quality of such data. The
second concerns the protection of those who acquire
the results of big data research. And finally it is always
also about the rights of those who are affected by the
assessment results in whatever way outside of contractual relationships.

2. THE LAW ON WARRANTY IN MODERN CODIFIED CIVIL LAW IS OUTDATED

The contractual rules on the protection of data
quality are obsolete.[4] They derive from 19th-century
commodity-oriented economic structures and safe-
guard at best exceptionally a liability in contractual or

quasi-contractual relationships. Accordingly the few published opinions on data quality in big data essentially only discuss the liability for transmission errors.[5]

The real test on the subject of information liability in the information society is that from now on data themselves are being made the subject of contracts. Traditionally, in what was then the only conceivable case of selling information in book form, the law proceeded on the basis that the contractually agreed use was hard to determine.[6] In law the buyer/reader of a book entertained no expectations of a book's content that were worthy of protection;[7] such expectations were as a rule only irrelevant desires for information.[8] Boundaries were only overstepped if a larger than average number of printing errors were present, pages were missing, or a statute book was completely obsolete.[9] Alternatively one worked with assurances and guarantees[10] or an independent consultancy agreement.[11] Otherwise there was the danger that the usually expected reliability of the actual facts would lead to a warranty irrespective of which party was at fault.[12]

The background to this restrictive attitude can be found in Art. 5 para. 3 clause 1 of the *Grun gesetz* (GG) [German Constitution] that privileges both the author of the book and its publisher.[13] From this the German Federal Court of Justice concludes that printing errors "can indeed be largely avoided by a customary and commercially generally acceptable method of production, although not with certainty. In individual cases, therefore, it may be that trade and communication does not and may not rely on the absence of a single such error."[14] Even if we recognize such privileging, this is not applied to data providers in the age of big data. At least, since the Law of Obligations reform, data are "other objects," according to Section 453 para. 1 (second alternative) BGB [German Civil Code], with the result that Sections 433 ff. BGB are correspondingly applicable.[15]

3. THE LAW OF TORTS IN THE BGB AND OTHERS IS ALSO WORTHLESS

As we can clearly see in the example of the German Civil Code, the rules of tort liability, too, are obsolete. The only provision is protection against a worst-case scenario in information law, the complete loss of data through the construct of a loss of property (Section 823 para. 1 BGB).[16]

Incidentally these are the dire consequences of the fact that the assessment of raw data, for example in the case of scoring, is seen as the creation and communication of value judgments, even in the opinion of the Federal Court of Justice. Thus Section 824 para. 1 BGB requires that untruthful statements are being disseminated, not just value judgments, according to the Court.[17] By contrast, the Court said, Section 824 para. 1 BGB offers no protection against pejorative expressions of opinion and value judgments. An exception would only come into force, according to the Court, "if during the expression, in the recipient's view the elements of the opinion fade into the background in the face of the underlying facts" (para. 11).

Equally, the Court said, the law concerning the right to carry on an established business cannot be of further help. For in the necessary weighing of interests in the context of Section 823 para. 1 BGB, it should be noted that Art. 5 para. 1 GG "does not prohibit the dissemination of true and objective information on the market, which can be important for the competitive behavior of market participants, even if the content has an adverse affect on individual competitive positions."[18]

These antiquated guidelines appear not only in Germany, but also, for example, in Anglo-American law, as a reading of the famous *Winter v. G.P. Putnam's Sons* of 1991 demonstrates.[19] In this case two mushroom enthusiasts sued for damages the publisher who had published the British book *The Encyclopedia of Mushrooms* in the USA. The book was a work of reference on the subject of collecting and preparing mushrooms that nevertheless contained erroneous and misleading information concerning the identification of highly toxic mushrooms. The plaintiffs trusted the book's descriptions, ate the mushrooms they had collected accordingly—mushrooms that turned out to be highly toxic—and became seriously ill. The plaintiffs based their claim on, among other things, "products liability," on "breach of warranty," and on "negligent misrepresentation," but without success.

The Court rejected the plaintiffs' view that this work of reference was a "product" in the meaning of the term "products liability,"[20] as only "items of a tangible nature"[21] are included in this term. In the case of the contents of books, the Court said, it was a question of non-tangible ideas, which were not comparable to "products" in the abovementioned sense. In addition, the Court said that no other judgment arose in consideration of the type of publication. Moreover any differentiation between the contents of guidebooks and encyclopedias and abstract ideas was illusory.[22]

The Court also rejected liability on the grounds of negligent misrepresentation. It said that although publishers had a fundamental duty to investigate the contents of their publications, insofar as there were no grounds, however, a further examination of the contents for its accuracy was not required.[23] In addition the Court rejected liability based on the law of warranty; for the abovementioned reasons the Court regarded it as unlikely that a book publisher would offer a warranty for the accuracy of the information.[24]

Another example worth mentioning on the question of tort liability of organs of the press is the case of *Alm v. Van Nostran⸱ Reinhol⸱ Co., Inc.*[25] Here the case involved instructions in the book *The Making of Tools*, published by the defendant. The plaintiff had incurred injuries while making a woodcarving tool as explained in the book, and brought a claim against the publisher. The plaintiff alleged "negligent misrepresentation" on the grounds that the defendant failed to verify the accuracy of the book's contents themselves, and independently of the author. The Court dismissed the claim, on the grounds of disproportionate scope of verification, as otherwise the publisher would be obliged to check all publications in detail and test them for their accuracy in order to prevent liability towards an unspecified number of people.[26]

Examining Anglo-American legislation[27] as well shows that the liability of publishers for published content from the point of view of data quality/

data accuracy is interpreted globally in a restricted way. Extending the journalistic duty of care to book publishers from this point of view would create a crass discrepancy with regard to the mass of published works, and could entail effects that might threaten their very existence:

> To impose the suggested broad legal duty upon publishers of nationally circulated magazines, newspapers and other publications, would not only be impractical and unrealistic, but would have a staggering adverse effect on the commercial world and our economic system. For the law to permit such exposure to those in the publishing business who in good faith accept paid advertisements for a myriad of products would open the doors "to a liability in an indeterminate amount for an indeterminate time to an indeterminate class."[28]

According to Anglo-American law, there is no fundamental distinction between liability for erroneous information in print and in digital form, and the applicability of each law of liability depends on the individual case.

4. THE RULES OF THE EU DATA PROTECTION DIRECTIVE ON DATA QUALITY

One initial fragmentary approach to a juristic validation of data quality is offered by Art. 6 (1) (d) of the
EU Data Protection Directive,[29] with its assertion
that data, insofar as they relate to a person, have to
be up-to-date and accurate ("accurate and, where
necessary, kept up to date"). Astonishingly this regulation has never been implemented in Germany, and
in this Germany remains almost alone in Europe. For
example, in Austria the provisions concerning quality
have been implemented in Section 6 of the Austrian
Data Protection Act. Switzerland has even extended
the regulations. According to Art. 5 of the Swiss Data
Protection Act, the processor of personal data has to
make sure of their accuracy. He must take all reasonable steps to correct or destroy data that are incorrect
or incomplete in light of the purpose of its collection
or processing.

In Great Britain the EU Data Protection Directive
was implemented as the 1998 Data Protection Act.
While the latter regulates the fundamentals of British
data protection law, a concretization of these rules
takes place through statutory instruments and regulations.[30] The 1998 Data Protection Act sets up a total of

eight data protection principles. The quality regulation in Art. 6 (1) (d) of the EU Data Protection Directive was implemented through the fourth data protection principle, which prescribes that personal data must be up-to-date and accurate.[31]

For reasons of practicability the Act provides special regulations for cases in which individuals provide information about themselves, or personal data is acquired from third parties. In these cases, even if personal data are factually inaccurate, this is not considered a breach of the fourth data protection principle if, in the case of the data subject or a third party false information was entered correctly, the data controller has taken reasonable steps to ensure the quality of the data, and the data indicate that the data subject has alerted the data controller to the inaccuracies.[32] What precisely is to be understood by "reasonable steps" depends on the kind of personal data, and on the importance of accuracy in each individual case.[33]

In the case of *Smeaton v. Equifax Plc*, the UK Court of Appeal pointed out that the 1998 Data Protection Act justified no absolute obligation to maintain the accuracy of personal data, but merely demanded the taking of reasonable steps to maintain data quality. This reasonableness is to be judged according to each individual case. The Court also said that the fourth data protection principle did not lead to a parallel obligation in the area of legal torts.[34]

The silence of civil law is particularly astonishing if we look at the current significance of Art. 6 of the EU Data Protection Directive in the discussion about legal policy. In its Google ruling, the European Court of Justice emphasized the principles of data quality, and not without cause. It said that any processing of personal data must comply with the principles established in Art. 6 of the Directive in relation to the quality of the data (para. 71).[35] On the principle of data accuracy the Court also said "even initially lawful processing of accurate data may, in the course of time, become incompatible with the directive where those data are no longer necessary in the light of the purposes for which they were collected or processed" (para. 93).

In the USA, the Data Quality Act (DQA), also known as the Information Quality Act (IQA), was adopted in 2001 as a component of the Consolidated Appropriations Act. It empowers the Office of Management and Budget to issue guidelines, which should guarantee and improve the quality and integrity of the information that is published by state institutions ("Guidelines for Ensuring and Maximizing the Quality, Objectivity, Utility, and Integrity of Information Disseminated by Federal Agencies"[36]).[37]

In addition mechanisms should be created that enable data subjects affected by the dissemination of false information to have this flagged up and corrected.[38]

A distinction between personal and non-personal data is not made in this case, however. In addition, the scope of the Data Quality Act is limited only to the dissemination of information by state authorities to the public.[39]

Furthermore there is no federal law that establishes guidelines for the data quality of personal data in the non-state domain. Since US data protection law is regulated by numerous laws and guidelines at both federal and state level, there are individual sector-specific laws that contain regulations touching on data quality (e.g. the Fair Credit Reporting Act or the 1996 Health Insurance Portability and Accountability Act). For example the Fair Credit Reporting Act requires users of consumer reports to inform consumers of their rights to contest the accuracy of reports concerning them. Another example is the HIPAA Security Rule according to which institutions concerned (e.g. health programs, settlement facilities in healthcare, or healthcare companies) must guarantee the integrity of electronically protected health data.[40]

The examples of the USA and the EU Data Protection Directive demonstrate that the growing relevance of data quality as an issue has at least been recognized. On the other hand veracity[41] of data can only be attained if effective tools are created that can ensure quality standards for data. Both the EU Directive and the Data Quality Act are giving a lead in the right direction.

However, the fact that up until now Germany has not implemented Art. 6 of the EU Data Protection Directive at a national level, and that the Data Quality Act in the US recognizes solely the dissemination of information by state institutions, nevertheless indicates that a need for correction and reform exists.

5. SCORING AND BIG DATA

A further element of a legal validation of data quality is provided by Section 28b of the German Federal Data Protection Act (BDSG) and its regulations on scoring. This offers a new criterion for the assessment of the way in which information is collected, namely the establishment of a scientifically recognized mathematical-statistical procedure for the calculation of probability value (no. 1).[42]

The scope of this regulation is unclear. It may be interpreted in such a way that it can be applied beyond the narrow discipline of financial scoring to profiling and other big data assessments as well. This is backed up, for example, by the Federal Government's justification of the draft legislation: "Scoring is a mathematical-statistical procedure that makes it possible to calculate the probability of a certain person demonstrating certain behavior."[43] There is absolutely no reference that says that scoring must be related and limited to credit checks. The only limitation contained in the regulation is the reference that scoring may be used "for the purpose of deciding on the creation, execution or termination of a contractual relationship with the data subject." Bringing the concept of probability values into play goes far beyond the usual procedure of credit scoring. For example, in all business transactions, prognoses inevitably have an influence on the decision concerning a business deal. In a similar way many big data processes are based on scoring that has an influence on the creation of differentiated business models (in the area of health insurance, for example).

This categorization has far-reaching consequences for the world of big data. According to Section 28b BDSG, the mathematical standards must be "demonstrably essential" for calculating the probability of the action. The reference to "demonstrability" shifts the burden of explanation and proof onto the big data analysts, and gives the data protection supervisory authority, under Section 38 (3) sentence 1 BDSG, the opportunity of being informed about the parameters of demonstrability in the case of the use of personal data.[44]

6. THE QUESTION OF DATA QUALITY IS NOT A PROBLEM OF DATA PROTECTION LEGISLATION

Notably, both specifications (Art. 6 of the EU Data Protection Directive and Section 28b BDSG) are incorrectly qualified as data protection legislation. The background to this is the deliberate legal confusion of consumer protection and data protection in such a way that data protection law becomes an extension of consumer protection law. However, questions as to the accuracy of data or the basis of scoring affect not only consumers but businesspeople as well. To that extent here, too, it is not a question of consumer protection, but of a general legal promotion of the accuracy of data analyses in light of big data.[45]

In this respect, scoring is by no means a question relating to the admissibility of the use of personal data, but rather to the accuracy of the relevant procedures and their results. However, data protection legislation has nothing to do with the question of the accuracy of data. Equally, consumer protection law does not address the central question of data accuracy: in the world of business in particular there is also a very pressing need for protection against the irresponsible use of big data tools. The guarantee of data quality is an issue of civil law in general.

In this respect, the BDSG legislates for a situation that dogmatically bypasses the objective of data protection law. Accordingly the objective of Section 38 BDSG is also incorrect, which in combination with Section 28b no. 1 is intended to enable the supervisory authority to understand the established context scientifically. The data protection supervisory authority is in no position to judge the mathematical-statistical validity of scoring procedures. It has never been their job, nor their core area of competence. In that case the data protection supervisory authority would obviously have had to employ mathematicians to check the validity, which would lead to additional administration costs, which, however, the government's draft of the then existing BDSG definitively excluded in its justification of Section 28b BDSG.[46]

7. THE QUESTION IS HOW DATA SHOULD BE COLLECTED IN THE INTEREST OF EVERYONE

The stereotypically defensive attitude against scoring/profiling makes the error of thinking that the issue of data accuracy must be of interest to all participants in the flow of data. In this respect it cannot be a question of fighting against scoring/profiling, but of promoting data accuracy within the scoring system. We achieve nothing by polemicizing against the overpowering hunger for data; rather we will have to regulate in a focused way on the "how" of data assessment in the context of today's data society.

8. IT IS NOT A QUESTION OF "RIGHT" OR "WRONG"

One idea might be to protect data quality through a connection to the relevant data quality standards, and to demand it through tough instruments of civil law. Categorizing data as "right" or "wrong" is not appropriate. Big data is concerned with correlations and probabilities, and is not suited to dualistic assertions of truth. But it is precisely in equating probabilities and facts that we find one of the biggest cases of liability in the debate about big data. As early as 2010, Danah Boyd, a renowned US sociologist, issued a warning about the tragic misunderstandings in this field: "Bigger data are not always better data."[47] And she warned justifiably:

> Interpretation is the hardest part of doing data analysis. And no matter how big your data is, if you don't understand the limits of it, if you don't understand your own biases, you will misinterpret it.

9. MODERN MODELS OF DATA QUALITY

It turns out to be disastrous that, after an initial period of activity, the discussion in IT about standards in data quality has died down once again. The 1990s gave birth to current data quality standards such as accuracy, consistency, timeliness, completeness, and uniqueness.[48] This debate continued until 2008 and led to the foundation of a Deutsche Gesellschaft für Datenqualität (DGDQ) [German Society for Data Quality] which was then *e facto* disbanded. Currently an ISO standard (ISO 8000)[49] is under consideration whose form cannot yet be determined.

Meanwhile the differentiation between five levels of quality has become standard: availability, usability, reliability, relevance, and presentation quality.[50] These five levels have formed the basis for Chinese researchers, for example, to summarize the current debate in the context of a highly differentiated model of the postulated standard:[51]

A universal, two-layer big data quality standard for assessment.

Dimensions	Elements	Indicators	
1) Availability	1) Accessibility	■	Whether a data access interface is provided
		■	Data can be easily made public or easy to purchase
	2) Timeliness	■	Within a given time, whether the data arrive on time
		■	Whether data are regularly updated
		■	Whether the time interval from data collection and processing to release meets requirements
2) Usability	1) Credibility	■	Data come from specialized organizations of a country, field, or industry
		■	Experts or specialists regularly audit and check the correctness of the data content
		■	Data exist in the range of known or acceptable values

3) Reliability	1) Accuracy	■	Data provided are accurate
		■	Data representation (or value) well reflects the true state of the source information
		■	Information (data) representation will not cause ambiguity
	2) Consistency	■	After data have been processed, their concepts, value domains, and formats still match as before processing
		■	During a certain time, data remain consistent and verifiable
		■	Data and the data from other data sources are consistent or verifiable
	3) Integrity	■	Data format is clear and meets the criteria
		■	Data are consistent with structural integrity
		■	Data are consistent with content integrity
	4) Completeness	■	Whether the deficiency of a component will impact use of the data for data with multi-components
		■	Whether the deficiency of a component will impact data accuracy and integrity

4) Relevance	1) Fitness		
		▪	The data collected do not completely match the theme, but they expound one aspect
		▪	Most datasets retrieved are within the retrieval theme users need
		▪	Information theme provides matches with users' retrieval theme
5) Presentation Quality	1) Readability	▪	Data (content, format, etc.) are clear and understandable
		▪	It is easy to judge that the data provided meet needs
		▪	Data description, classification, and coding content satisfy specification and are easy to understand

This model highlights the complexity of quality assurance in the case of big data. What is required here is not only the accuracy of the input data (mentioned here under point 3.1 "Accuracy"), but rather that the entire procedure from the inputting of data to the presentation of the final data correlations must be structured appropriately.

Under "availability" they distinguish between "accessibility" of data and "timeliness." The authors measure accessibility using indicators such as being able to access data through an interface and the possibility of receiving data free of charge or at a reasonable price. They would like to ensure timeliness using procedures that guarantee the regular updating of input data, and an appropriate projection of the time periods from input via processing to output. Usability, too, must be ensured, for example through regular auditing by experts or by examination of the source of input data. Moreover, we should note that they demand not only the relevance of the output (its "fitness for purpose"), but that emphasis is placed on "readability" as well—the intelligibility of the output and its presentation in a way that avoids misunderstandings.

10. INPUT, PROCESSING, OUTPUT—AND LIABILITY

It is particularly important to revisit the old debates on data quality in light of big data, as the output of a big data assessment can be disastrous if the data entered are assessed incorrectly, twice over, or inconsistently. This is what gives rise to factually incorrect results on the basis of mathematically correct and apparently clean methods.

An efficient legal system would be able to distinguish between input, processing, and output. The input would have to meet classic contractually binding data quality standards that have an influence on the contractual relationship between data sellers and buyers in the form of the usual stipulated conditions. This includes above all the aforementioned criteria of availability. In the contractual relationship between big data analyst and big data customer the classic data quality criteria equally apply, in particular the "fitness test" as is usually required. In relation to interested third parties, the infringement of the data quality standards as per Sections 823 (1), 824 BGB in the context of the test for negligence would apply. This would presume that during big data processing a record of the tools used would be required analogous to Section 28b BDSG, and that big data companies must reveal the basis of their assessment of individual data to their customers and interested parties.[52]

Notes

1. For example Xiaofeng Meng and Xiang Ci, "Big Data Management: Concepts, Techniques and Challenges" in *Journal of Computer Research and Development 50* (2013), pp. 146–69. But the debate is different, however, in certain areas such as aeronautical data where the data quality is regulated and standardized extensively. See Annex IV ("Data quality requirements") of EU Commission Regulation no. 73/2010 of January 26, 2010 for the qualitative requirements in aeronautical data and aeronautical information for the entirety of European airspace, http://eur-lex.europa.eu/legal-content/EN/TXT/HTML/?uri=CELEX:32010R0073&from=DE.

2. Declan Butler, "When Google Got Flu Wrong" in *Nature* 494 (2013), pp. 155, 155–6. Equally shocking in this respect is Sharona Hoffman's empirical study on the deficiencies in data quality in the medical world. Sharona Hoffman, "Medical Big Data and Big Data Quality Problems" in *Connecticut Insurance Law Journal* 21 (2014), pp. 289 ff.

3. Helmut Martin-Jung, "Warum wir Big Data verstehen müssen" in *Süddeutsche Zeitung*, October 10, 2015.

4. The following ideas are based on the premises of German civil law. However the legal position in other EU Member States is no better.

5. See Christopher Peschel and Sebastian Rockstroh, "Big Data in der Industrie – Chancen und Risiken neuer datenbasierter Dienste" in MMR (2014), p. 571.

6. BGH NJW (1988), p. 2597; also Johannes Wertenbruch, "Gewährleistung beim Kauf von Kunstgegenständen nach neuem Schuldrecht" in NJW (2004), pp. 1977, 1979 f. Helmut Haberstumpf, "Verkauf immaterieller Güter" in NJOZ (2015), pp. 793, 796, maintains that only tangible property can be the starting point for a product purchase.

7. Harm Peter Westermann, "Münchener Kommentar zum Bürgerlichen Gesetzbuch" in BGB, 7th edn. (2015), para. 73.

8. BGH NJW (1958), p. 138.

9. AG Stuttgart NJW-RR (1995), p. 565; see also Bamberger/ Roth/Faust, para 70; Ulrich Foerste, "Die Produkthaftung für Druckwerke" in NJW (1991), pp. 1433, 1436; *Soergel/ Huber,* 12th edn., Section 459 (old version) para. 344.

10. BGH in NJW (1973), p. 843; criticized in Soergel/Huber, note 19.

11. BGHZ 70, 356 = NJW (1978), p. 997; cf. for more detail Johannes Köngen, "Die Haftung von Börseninformationsdiensten" in JZ (1978), p. 389; Christine von Hertzberg, *Die Haftung von Börseninformationsdiensten*

(Heidelberg: Fachmedien Recht und Wirtschaft in Deutscher Fachverlag GmbH, 1987).

12. Westermann, see note 7.

13. See criticism in Foerste, "Die Produkthaftung für Druckwerke", pp. 1433, 1434.

14. BGH, NJW 1970, 1963.

15. RegE, BT-Drs. 14/6040, p. 24; Joachim Jickeli and Malte Stieper in Staudinger, BGB, rev. edn. (2011), BGB Section 90 para. 17; Roland Michael Beckmann in Staudinger, BGB, rev. edn. (2014), Section 453 para. 37. Also OLG Düsseldorf, judgment of February 17, 2010 – 17 U 167/09 in BeckRS (2010), 09514; LG Munich I, judgment of December 10, 2008 – 16 HK O 10382/08 in BeckRS (2009), 88429.

16. OLG Karlsruhe, judgment of November 7, 1995 – 3 U 15/95 in CR (1996), 32.

17. Judgment of February 22, 2011, ref. VI ZR 120/10, NJW (2011), p. 2204. See criticism in Thilo Weichert, "Scoring in Zeiten von Big Data" in ZRP (2014), pp. 168, 170 f.

18. Judgment of February 22, 2011, see note 17.

19. *Winter v. G.P. Putnam's Sons* – 938 F.2d 1033 (9th Cir. 1991); see also *Jones v. J.B. Lippincott Co.*, 694 F. Supp. 1216, 15 Media L. Rep. 2155.

20. Cf. Section 402A of the Restatement (Second) of Tort.

21. *Winter v. G.P. Putnam's Sons*, 938 F.2d 1033 (1034).

22. *Winter v. G.P. Putnam's Sons*, 938 F.2d 1033 (1036).

23. *Winter v. G.P. Putnam's Sons*, 938 F.2d 1033 (1037).

24. *Winter v. G.P. Putnam's Sons*, 938 F.2d 1033 (1038).

25. *Alm v. Van Nostran Reinhol Co., Inc.*, 480 N.E.2d 1263 (Ill. App. 1 Dist., 1985).

26. *Alm v. Van Nostran Reinhol Co., Inc.*, 480 N.E.2d 1263, (1264).

27. *Winter v. G.P. Putnam's Sons*, 938 F.2d; *Alm v. Van Nostran⟨ Reinhol⟨ Co., Inc.*, 480 N.E.2d 1263; *Jones v. JB. Lippincott Co.*, 694 F. Supp. 1216 (D. Md., 1988).

28. *Yuhas v. Mu⟨ge* (1974), 129 N.J. Super. 207, 209–10, 322 A.2d 824, 825; accord *Suarez v. Un⟨erwoo⟨* (1980), 103 Misc.2d 445, 426 N.Y.S.2d 208.

29. This regulation can be found in almost identical form in Art. 5 of the draft of the EU General Data Protection Regulation.

30. http://unitedkingdom.taylorwessing.com/uploads/tx_siru-plawyermanagement/

NB_000168_Overview_UK_data_protection_law_WEB.pdf (last accessed on 25.11.2015).

31. Sch. 1 pt. 1 para. 4 Data Protection Act (1998); detailed information on the fourth principle of data protection: https://ico.org.uk/for-organisations/guide-to-data-protection/principle-4-accuracy/ (last accessed on 25.11.2015).

32. Sch. 1 pt. 2 para. 7 Data Protection Act (1998).

33. https://ico.org.uk/for-organisations/guide-to-data-protection/principle-4-accuracy/ (last accessed on 25.11.2015).

34. *Smeaton v. Equifax Plc* (2013), EWCA Civ 108, http://www.bailii.org/ew/cases/EWCA/Civ/2013/108.html (last accessed on 25.11.2015).

35. Cf. judgments concerning Österreichischer Rundfunk et al., EU:C:2003:294, para. 65; ASNEF and FECEMD, C468/10 and C469/10, EU:C:2011:777, para. 26, and Worten, C342/12, EU:C:2013:355, para. 33.

36. https://www.whitehouse.gov/omb/fedreg_final_information_quality_guidelines/ (last accessed on 25.11.2015).

37. https://www.whitehouse.gov/omb/fedreg_reproducible (last accessed on 25.11.2015).

38. Subsection (2) (B) of the DQA.

39. A. Dallas Wait and John P. Maney, "Regulatory Science and the Data Quality Act" in *Environmental Claims Journal*, p. 148.

40. Rosemary P. Jay (ed.), *Data Protection & Privacy 2015*, (London: Law Business Research Ltd., 2015), pp. 210f.

41. Referring to Tyler Douglas's "Four Vs of Big Data" (volume, variety, velocity, and veracity).

42. See also Anders Härting's early ideas on this topic: http://www.cr-online.de/blog/2015/05/20/vier-the-sen-zur-neu-entbrannten-scoring-debatte/

43. BT-Drs. 16/10 529, pp. 1 f.

44. To this extent it is regrettable that precisely this component of Section 28b BDSG is not to be incorporated into the EU's General Data Protection Regulation. According to suggestions made by the Commission, Parliament and Council on Art. 20 DCGVO, first of all an "automatic decision" (Council) or "measure" (Commission) should be provided based on profiling that is "profiling which leads to measures producing legal effects concerning the data subject or does similarly significantly affect the interests, rights or freedoms of the concerned data subject" (European Parliament).

45. Anders Härting, see note 42. BT-Drs. 16/10 529, p. 1 f.

46. BT-Drs 16/12011, p. 18 below.

47. Danah Boyd, "Privacy and Publicity in the Context of Big Data" in *WWW*, Raleigh, North Carolina, April 2010, http://www.danah.org/papers/talks/2010/WWW2010.html

48. Bernd Heinrich and Mathias Klier, "Datenqualitätsmetriken für ein ökonomisch orientiertes Qualitätsmanagement" in Knut Hildebrand, Marcus Gebauer, Holger Hinrichs and Michael Mielke (eds.), *Daten- un♦ Informationsqualität: Auf ♦em Weg zur Information Excellence* 2nd edn. (2012), pp. 49–66; Bernd Heinrich,

Marcus Kaiser, and Mathias Klier, "*How to Measure Data Quality? A Metric-base¹ Approach*" in *28th International Conference of Information Systems (ICIS)*, 2007.

49. J.L. Wang, H. Li and Q. Wang, "Research on ISO 8000 Series Standards for Data Quality" in *Stan¹ar¹ Science* 12 (2010), pp. 44–6.

50. Cinzia Cappiello, Chiara Francalanci, and Barbara Pernici, "Data Quality Assessment from User's Perspective" in *Proce¹ures of the 2004 International Workshop on Information Quality in Information Systems* (New York: ACM, 2004), pp. 78 ff.

51. Li Cai and Yangyong Zhu, "The Challenges of Data Quality and Data Quality Assessment in the Big Data Era", http://datascience.codata.org/article/10.5334/dsj-2015-002/

52. Cf. the US perspective in Omer Tene and Jules Polonetksy, "Big Data for All: Privacy and User Control in the Age of Analytics" in *Northwestern Journal of Technology an¹ Intellectual Property* 11, 5, (2013), pp. 239, 270 ff. On the "Big Data Disclosure Problem" see also Michael Mattioli, "Disclosing Big Data" in *Minnesota Law Review* 99 (2014–15), pp. 535 ff.

CHAPTER 9

ART, HOLACRACY, AND THE TRANSFORMATION OF POWER STRUCTURES

HANS ULRICH OBRIST AND SIMON DENNY

Hans Ulrich Obrist conﬂucteﬂ this interview with Simon Denny on a ﬂight from Beijing to Hong Kong.

Hans-Ulrich Obrist: The topic of power, visibility, the invisibility of power is something British documentary film-maker Adam Curtis addresses a lot in his films.

Simon Danny: Yes.

HUO: What do you see as the most apt visualization of power, Simon? Because obviously in your current exhibition at the Serpentine Sackler Gallery "Products for Organising," you look at it in terms of products for organizing. I was looking for a sense of how you connect to Holacracy here. Holacracy is a shift of power. Can you tell us a little bit about that?

SD: That is an interesting question. Holacracy is a formalized organizational structure, a management strategy that works with a fully orchestrated management-wide situation, but it also tries to take a hierarchy and flip it upside down. So the hierarchy is no longer a triangle with the boss at the top and the workers further down the chain; it's more like a visualization of different intersecting circles with people acting in different roles. It acts to redistribute power across the organization and enable people as if they were all entrepreneurs, as if it wasn't employees who were working in the factory, but everybody who was also owning a part of the organization was working as if they were part of that managerial class.

HUO: On the cover of your Serpentine book, *Pro∤ucts for Organising*, there is indeed the word Holacracy and you connect it...

SD: Not to anarchy.

HUO: The image you use looks like a nest of circles. What exactly is Holacracy? How would you define it and how does it differentiate itself from anarchy and to what extent is it a nest of circles?

SD: Holacracy can be visualized as a nest of interlocking circles. Instead of job descriptions employees have roles and they act within circles of people instead of teams. It means that people on the front line, where they have a decision-making process, are making the decisions rather than a manager or a boss further up the chain. In the book by the founder of Holacracy, Brian Robertson,[1] he describes his experience of piloting an airplane. Everything on the airplane, all the signals on the instruments in the cockpit, were telling him everything was okay except one flashing light. He thought that was a very insignificant flashing light so he ignored it, but actually that was the one thing that was telling him he was about to crash. So that was the whole thing: an inspiration for Holacracy, giving everybody within the organization power to make a decision where they have the knowledge, rather than other people further up the chain not being able to do the same thing. What I found interesting was the knowledge that it works in a shoe store company such as the Amazon-owned Zappos with headquarters in Las Vegas, but also in GCHQ, the British version of the NSA, which is in the public sector. So there's public sector, private sector, a sales force, and a security agency, both working with the distributed authority model.

HUO: So can we say Holacracy is everywhere?

SD: Holacracy is everywhere and the idea of redistributing power within organizations is a very powerful one right now.

HUO: You also added a printed sticker which says "actively manage culture and empower others to own it." To what extent does Holacracy do this? There obviously lies this idea within it that ownership becomes more horizontal.

SD: That's the thing. Exactly.

HUO: Is it a kind of a *Genossenschaft*, because in a way Migros, the famous Swiss supermarket chain, is a *Genossenschaft*, it belongs to everyone, it belongs to the people.

SD: Right, exactly.

HUO: Is it a model of *Genossenschaft?*

SD: I think it's an attempt to take a *Genossenschaft* model and apply it to a commercializable product that can apply to a lot of different kinds of organizations. But I think *Genossenschaft* can't always work within particular kinds of structures. It's the idea of managing culture—and culture is a powerful metaphor for the way that people work together within institutions and within organizations. So that sticker that you mentioned, that's from Zappos. The Zappos CEO, Tony Hsieh, is the poster boy for Holacracy and is actively managing culture and distributing culture across his organization in the way that it looks and the way that the office is designed and the way that the building is used, so that people collide with each other and interact with each other in a small amount of space. This all comes together to make a Holacratic organization possible.

HUO: I also wanted to ask you about the notion of "agile," because the word "agile" appears on quite a lot of your sculptures and it's basically very much part also of the floor plan of the exhibition. It's an agile floor plan, so it's part of the architecture, it's embedded. How is the notion of "agile" connected to Holacracy? Can you tell us about the agile age of Holacracy, in the context of this Convoco conversation?

SD: Absolutely. "Agile" is another managerial trend at the moment which is derived from programming languages. If Holacracy is seen as an operating system for an organization I guess "agile" maybe represents the original operating system for an organization. It focusses on keeping everything flexible, keeping space flexible, keeping people flexible, keeping processes flexible so you respond to change. Instead of following your brief you work with people through processes. This drives an organization that can change very quickly with the times. This can expand out into an office environment and can be expressed physically.

Agile space is also being theorized and implemented in Zappos and GCHQ. Certain desk arrangements can make agile space more possible and make companies more flexible and more agile. It's a sort of operating system and this computer metaphor, this programming metaphor for management, is coming across from modern tech institutions.

HUO: Obviously the notion of the agile embraces and drives change. I suppose "agile" is also connected to this idea of permanent change.

SD: Exactly. If we acknowledge that that's the case, and if we acknowledge that we want our organizations to be relevant and to adapt to the times that we're living in, and we want to graft onto them different ways of constantly changing, then "agile" is the perfect framework to do that under. It's interesting that it comes from a programming context, but it's used both within commercial and public institutions and organizations, and it's used from a hacking space to a security space to a sales space. This puts all of those things in a similarly agile world where all of those things become part of the same flow.

HUO: You defined Holacracy beautifully earlier: how would you define "agile"?

SD: "Agile" is a flexible process for following management strategies and bringing people together in organizations.

HUO: We spoke about horizontal management structures and "agile." We spoke earlier today about fluidity and the notion of power being seen as something fluid that is not bound to certain institutions and individuals but sits more in a conversation space or in a space of argumentation, that is of who has the better argument. Can you tell us a little bit about this idea of fluid power in relation to your work?

SD: I'm always interested in seeing how fluid power can manifest itself visually with artists and diagrammatic structures as well. I try to distil or focus on those who have distilled these into images and diagrams and try to make sense out of those types of things. One of the questions here as well is whether management structures such as Holacracy really do away with power structures.

HUO: Exactly. Because again that's obviously Adam Curtis's argument when he says that power doesn't go away, but just becomes invisible.

SD: Right. I think you could definitely make that argument. I think one of the criticisms that's been held against Holacracy is this idea that if you empower workers to behave as if they own the business, to have a more incentivized stake in what they're doing, to feel like they're the managers of themselves, it also actually means you're just increasing productivity without giving anybody a stake. So this is a trick in some people's minds. I think that Holacracy is a really great attempt at solving a problem of distributing power and making decision-making structures reflect reality, but, of course, it doesn't come without problems.

HUO: Paul Klee famously said that art makes the invisible visible. That's very true for you because you basically make these invisible powers in a way visible. You create visualizations of Holacracy, of "agile," and of this new invisible power. One thing you visualized so strikingly is Kim Dotcom, the businessman living in New Zealand. Can you tell us a little bit about the invisible, visible power of Kim Dotcom?

SD: I think that was an amazing curatorial exercise in a way, when the US government selected and seized several things from Kim's collection, when they arrested him for megaupload.com. For me that was an amazing visualization of a certain argument about privacy, ownership, and sovereignty. When the US said we want to take these things off you they kind of sub-curated his collection. The US government and the US justice system curated a famous entrepreneur's collection of goods. I felt that bringing those together as an exhibition visualized that argument and visualized that conversation around who owns what, who has access to what, and how we can see it.

HUO: You once told me in an interview we did together that technology displaces experience and also displaces space and even time. So in a way it of course also displaces power. Can you tell us a little bit about why you think it displaces power? Because obviously in our investigation into this idea of power, visibility, and visibility displacement it is interesting to look at your work with Samsung, which is a technology company under new management. Maybe it's a moment, in terms of the displacement of power, to talk about "New Management."

SD: I think technology can displace power in all sorts of ways. It can also obscure the structures of power or reconfigure the structures of power. It can promise a voice to people like Facebook does, and Sheryl Sandberg said at DLD [Digital-Life-Design] 2012 that Facebook was providing people with a voice. But one could also argue it does the opposite, that a voice is heard in a cacophonic group that is then disempowered at the same time as they're empowered. I mean this is the one thing that technology can do.

The "New Management" exhibition that I did at Portikus, which then travelled to other venues, as well as the exhibition on Europe that you curated in Oslo—that was a way to show a pivot in managerial direction, a way to show a mirror reflecting back on the world of Lee Kun-hee, the powerful chairman of Samsung. It was about how one primarily domestic actor had ambitions to take over the world. They made a monument out of a meeting room in Frankfurt, into which they flew all of their top executives. They then took a Canaletto painting that was hanging in that space and made a monument to change, a monument to expansion, and a monument to global ambition, which I then had to surreptitiously re-make, because it's a private, executive monument to those ideas that can only be viewed by people within Samsung. I wanted to make such an important cultural monument more accessible to the rest of the world. So I re-made their monument, their "Frankfurt Declaration" monument to new management, to expansion, and to ambition, so that it was visible to the whole world. So power structures that were for executives, made by executives, became more accessible to people under the guise of art.

HUO: What do you think of this 1993 declaration by Samsung, which is of course at the center of the "New

Management" piece, with regard to this dialectic of power and powerlessness?

SD: I think that in a way they made a certain interior design stand in for that—a certain group of paintings, certain images—for the idea of aggressive expansion. But then they took that as an internal dialogue and the way that I forced it into being a more public dialogue shows just how carefully controlled and carefully managed the display of managerial power can be.

HUO: Historically the media have shaped political power—we could go into that further. When we talk about invisibility and Paul Klee's art making the invisible visible, this leads us also to your New Zealand Pavilion at the Marciana Library and Marco Polo Airport. It's very interesting because you connected the exhibition at the library and an airport at the 56th Biennale in Venice this year with this whole "Secret Power" idea, which looks into the geographic and political and intelligent visualization of the Snowden leaks. It looks into the library as an allegory of the value of knowledge. It then has different crossovers, but in the middle of it is David Darchicourt, the former Creative Director of NSA.

SD: Yes, exactly.

HUO: A very secret reference. Can you tell us a little bit about the power of the powerless and about "Secret Power," and how you make that visible in your two Venice pavilions?

SD: After I read *Secret Power*, a book by Nicky Hager, the famous New Zealand journalist, and after we saw the Snowden releases and saw all the visual language in those NSA slides, I wanted to imagine an artistic figure, an authorial figure for those slide drawings and for the illustrations that the NSA use to embody and visualize surveillance and power.

David Darchicourt was the Creative Director of the NSA. I found his images on his LinkedIn profile. I was trying to imagine an authorial figure and here suddenly somebody was promoting himself as he who used to be in charge of making all the images and drawings, or some of the images and drawings within the NSA.

So I translated his images and put them into giant vitrines and contrasted them against images of artists who were making the value of knowledge visible in Venetian times—Titian, Veronese, and Sansovino, who made this beautiful library. I contrasted David

Darchicourt's work with theirs, trying to imagine a historical lineage for the idea of visualizing intelligence.

HUO: Obviously on the one hand it seems that powerful and wealthy institutions such as the NSA can use data and surveillance technology to become more powerful, but can technology help us to look at and unlock the concentration of power and wealth in the world? Is data the new currency of power, and do those who hold the greatest amount of data hold the greatest power?

SD: I think you could definitely make that argument. I think the idea of data centers and data swarms and also a physical infrastructure of the Internet—who can have access to that, who can have direct access to that, who can hold that, who can make sense of it—is the key not only to geopolitical power at the moment but also to governance and who can have the most knowledge to govern the world. I mean that's a bit overgeneralized, but I think there's definitely a great point there.

HUO: I want to talk a little bit more about "Secret Power," because the exhibition at the Venice Biennale was a very multi-layered show connected to the architecture of this library. There were many, many

TRANSFORMATION OF POWER STRUCTURES

different vitrines and each vitrine had a story. Can you tell us about some of these stories because they're also about power?

SD: I wanted to try and find this artistic author, this artist figure at the NSA, who had made these drawings which are some of the most powerful drawings of power that exist today symbolizing the different surveillance programs which became so controversial after Snowden's leaks. I wanted to know who drew them, why they drew them and what role those drawings were playing in the lives of the secret powers at the intelligence agencies. I found this guy, David Darchicourt, whom I engaged in a number of ways. I copied all his work that he had on his public profile online, on LinkedIn.

HUO: With his agreement?

SD: No, without his agreement. Then I also got him to do some new work for me by using my designer friend, David Bennewith. Bennewith commissioned a new map from him and also a dinosaur in the style of some work that he'd done before the NSA. So we had some new commissions, a whole portfolio of his work, and we contrasted those with drawings taken from the Snowden slides. Then Charlotte Higgins from the *Guardian* came and saw the exhibition. She had a look at all the vitrines and then she called David Darchicourt and told him that he was the star of the show and being compared to Titian, Veronese, and Fra Mauro, the mapmaker, and that he was being reimagined as a contemporary artist. He said that he was flattered and that as long as his work was being acknowledged and his name was put forward with all his work then he was a happy man. He also described his work as a kind of a freelancer.

It was really interesting that there was a resonance between the older imagery from the Renaissance painters and the newer imagery from the NSA. In both, magicians came up a lot, these bearded wise men. On the one hand you had old depictions of philosophers in Renaissance paintings and in the NSA you had these game-like, fantasy-like cartoons that derived from magic and other types of contemporary card games. Then you also had contemporary magicians such as Teller from Penn & Teller, and these all came up as an imagining of a special cyber-magician.

HUO: You also had the CryptoKids.

SD: David Darchicourt did the CryptoKids for the public-facing museum of the NSA. They are cartoon characters, anthropomorphic animals that stand in for the role of different workers in the NSA. We see fantastic animals from the ceiling and the paintings on the ceiling and the celestial globes of Coronelli that had a resonance with some of these more cartoon-like, more illustrative diagrams that David Darchicourt was drawing.

HUO: In terms of power what about LinkedIn?

SD: LinkedIn was where we found David Darchicourt's profile, so in a way this personal disclosure of a career also becomes a way of mapping a secret network. It's really interesting the way that people who work in supposedly secret associations such as the NSA often put all their work histories online. It's very easy, if you spend enough time, to map out a group of co-workers from the way that they're working within these institutions. The public display of things on social media undermines the secrecy of the government agency.

HUO: There is also your "Innovator's Dilemma" exhibition at MoMA PS1 this year. To what extent does that connect to the question of power or non-power?

SD: That show looked at the way that commercial organizations or tech organizations present themselves to the world and the language and imagery they use. It brought them together as an art fair. I had a trade-fair booth for each show and brought together the different ways in which particular organizations communicate themselves to the world. You've got an overview of tech and the way that it orchestrates itself, the way that it communicates itself, and in a way the power of marketing and PR in forming public opinion.

HUO: One last question—the unrealized project. 2015 was such an extraordinary year for you with so many realized projects, the Venice Biennale, the Pavilion, the MoMA PS1 and the Serpentine show, a trip to China. What is still unrealized? What projects have been too big to be realized or too small to be realized? What are Simon Denny's unbuilt roads?

SD: I really want to make a public sculpture with the editor of *Business Insider*. I want to do a *Business Insider* public sculpture downtown, near Wall Street.

HUO: What interests you about *Business Insider*?

SD: *Business Insider* made me feel included in the financial world. It made me feel part of the club. Because I don't know anything about finance and it's a world that I really want to know about. *Business Insider* makes it fun and accessible and I feel like they'd be good at designing a monument downtown that would make finance fun and accessible to people down there as well. That would be something that I think would be worthwhile in New York.

Note

1. Brian Robertson is a businessman, CEO, and pioneer of business management. His software company has won many awards for its rapid growth and innovative employee management. *Forbes* and *Fast Company* credit him with the development of Holacracy.

CHAPTER 10

THOUGHTS ON CONTROLLING POWER

CHRISTOPH G. PAULUS

Power and powerlessness, it seems, are interdependent. Unlimited power exists only rarely, if at all, and is usually limited in time. Behind the apparent contradiction of the phrase "the powerlessness of power; the power of powerlessness" [translator's note: the translation of the German title of Convoco 2015] lies the description of an ancient phenomenon, namely that fear and trepidation in the face of power are combined with the admiration of power. This ambivalence leads to the situation where the extension of power regularly goes hand in hand with the attempt to contain it. There are extreme, disastrous instances that seem to contradict this symbiosis: for example, Caesar or Napoleon, or much worse and more inhuman cases such as Hitler or Ceauşescu or North Korea today. But, retrospectively at least, all these concentrations of power prove to be temporary phenomena against which opposition was mustered, and which were stemmed by the resulting build-up of power.

A. THOUGHTS ON THE ASSESSMENT OF POWER

Philosophers have been concerned with the phenomenon of power since time immemorial, so it seems fitting that we should first address what we understand by power and where its ambivalence lies. Within the current context, however, it goes without saying that such a discussion would be at best scratching the surface. Consequently it must suffice to understand power, as Max Weber says, as "the probability that one actor within a social relationship will be in a position to carry out his own will despite resistance."[1]

This definition is illuminating in its objective description of power as a relationship based on supremacy, and at the same time it addresses the subjective aspect of power in the notion of "resistance."

This latter aspect is significant as the ambivalence of power does not play out in objective reality. Here, at least in many cases, the power relations are clear, possibly and precisely because there is a struggle. On the other hand, whether power is considered as something positive or negative can only rarely be reduced to a common denominator. For example, think of the power that the Dalai Lama has as seen by the Chinese government on the one hand, and on the other in the eyes of the general (and above all Western) public. Or the power of a Kim Jong-un, who is cheered on by the scant upper classes of North Korean society but condemned by the broad mass of the population (and with them large portions of the world). Or the power of the Church, the power of Islamic imams, and the power of a Mahatma Gandhi.

As diverse and multifaceted as these examples are, they all prove the relativity of our assessment of power. What appears wonderful and worth protecting to one individual—perhaps even to the majority of people—and whose binding nature is desired by all parties, is abhorrent to another individual. In view of the plurality of values in the Western world in particular, there should only be a few forms of power, if any, that are regarded as positive by the population as a whole. Opposition can be found everywhere, towards everything and everyone. This, however, lays the groundwork for controlling power. For, as in Max Weber's words quoted above, defeated resistance only gives in to its fate very unwillingly for purely human reasons. Periodically, it will think about revenge, about a change in the prevailing power relations.

If we continually consider this scenario in its historical dimension, we see a kind of *perpetuum mobile* that has actually characterized communities across the world for centuries in the form of feuds, and still characterizes them today to some extent. We can see this when we follow Brendan Simms' arguments and observations in his stimulating book *Europe: The Struggle for Supremacy, 1453 to the Present.*[2] In his book, this period of around 550 years is characterized by a continually changing wrestling match for supremacy, but also for its control. As a result, when discussing power, both in the interpersonal and geopolitical contexts, one always immediately encounters attempts to control power. It is like a prism where the apparent opposites of power and powerlessness meet and mirror each other.

B. CONTROLLING

In considering the notion of the feud, it is legitimate to use this phenomenon as the crystallization point of any kind of nation building.[3] In legal history, it is generally accepted (and with good reason) that the formation of a state and of state power is at least (probably even essentially) connected with harnessing, containing, and suppressing for the benefit of the community the anxieties and uncertainties caused by centuries of feuds. But how can one enact this power to push through what is desired against the resistance of those pursuing feuds?

One can imagine various methods of doing this. Of course they are dependent on their respective power positions which can perhaps be subdivided as follows: power positions that cannot be controlled at all or only with the use of extreme brutality; and those whose control can be achieved in a civilized manner.

1. As far as the first category is concerned, there exist power positions that are considered God-given, and therefore unshakeable. Rebelling against them or suppressing them is thus almost out of the question. A good example is the latest Greek crisis. From the start it was tackled as a payments crisis that made the

topic of state insolvency law almost socially acceptable. In the course of the rescue package, Greece saw itself more and more in the position of a country that had been delivered up helplessly to the creditor powers, the all-too-familiar "Troika." The group of creditors imposed measures on Greece that brought the country to the brink of social and political bankruptcy. All this is well known.

But Greece had a position of power that was and is unshakeable, and which was present as an undertone at all the negotiations like the elephant in the room (and was thus certainly known to all participants), but which astonishingly was never publicly articulated. Powerless Greece's position of power results on the one hand from its geographical position in Southeast Europe, and on the other from the fact that during all the crisis years up to this point, Erdoğan's Turkey had been and is still moving in a new direction, whose goals are regarded with increasing skepticism in the geopolitical sphere of power. Against this backdrop the financial crisis appears in a different light, and it also explains many political inferences coming from Moscow and the interest of the US President in favor of debt cancellation. The geostrategic aim in this crisis is that Europe's southeast flank must be secure and remain so.

This example shows that there actually do exist positions of power that are unshakeable. If one wants to create friction with them, another battlefield must be chosen. A comparable God-given situation can also exist in the form of ideas—or, more precisely, the people who embody them. Victor Hugo summed this up in the timeless phrase: "Nothing is more powerful than an idea whose time has come."[4] He who espouses such an idea benefits from the tailwind that also bestows a supra-personal position of power, such as Greece's geostrategic position. To want to control such a burgeoning idea is naturally an increasingly observable phenomenon that is all the more understandable as its power can regularly only be verified in hindsight, *ex-post*, while at the moment it emerges, by contrast, it is perhaps only one oppositional idea among many others. Accordingly the attempt to control this power typically proceeds by increasing step by step, and the sanctions become more severe the more successfully the idea and its representatives make progress.

A final example of this category can be found in the person of the aforementioned Dalai Lama. Regarded as apparently powerless as an individual, he is arguably the only person against whom China is waging a campaign. China's government is doing everything conceivable to suppress and eliminate the power of his charisma—which they fear—and thus his person. Anyone visiting Tibet and being reminded of the country's history by comparison[5] will easily recognize the brutality used in the attempt to break the power of this religious leader. The paradox in this situation is that the power of the Dalai Lama actually only derives from the fact that he is being attacked by China in this way. Or to put it another way, the more powerless the Dalai Lama is rendered by these attacks, the more powerful he seems to become.

2. The second category of power distinguishes itself particularly from the first in that in this case the idea of God-givenness is absent. Instead we are dealing with positions of power that were man-made. Even if the possibilities of control seem easier, the struggle to maintain power even in these cases is multifaceted and intense.

In the first instance we can assert that philosophy, for example, has always tried to control this form of power. When Plato and Aristotle wrote discourses on how a state should ideally be formed and governed, they did so in an attempt and with the desire that the assigned positions of power be channeled along predetermined lines to make them work optimally for the benefit of all. Fundamentally this is educational literature, which can be categorized in a wider literary context alongside works that deal with the "education of the human race."[6] The aim of all these writings is to influence people to live together in harmony; through insight and reason the power of each individual should be channeled along the right paths that are welcomed by all. The only apparent counter-example is Machiavelli's *The Prince*: this is just a description of actualities, with the result that reasons of state replace an ethical postulate.

Whether mere pragmatism or idealism, power should not be exercised in an unfettered way, but should be subordinated to a predetermined, higher goal. Especially during periods of predominantly absolutist domination—from an historical point of view—such writings are of course (also) attempts to control power. These attempts are particularly difficult if the ruler sees or suggests his power as God-given or God-derived, as this allows the ruler to legitimize his own display of power in a particularly effective way. If needs be the appeal to reason and insight helps, besides the use of force.

From a legal point of view, though, attempts to control power are far and away more significant if they are undertaken by means of the law. It is indeed possible that it was a concern of the law from the very beginning to rein in power. Notwithstanding the attempt, which can be observed repeatedly in the past and today, to use the law precisely to strengthen one's own power, the law's range of instruments has also time and again been characterized by limitation. Probably because of this characteristic, almost all dictators in history, from Nero to Hitler, have always tried to present even their most evil excesses of power as sanctioned by law, thus conferring absolution on even their worst misdeeds.

We must confine ourselves to just a few examples to provide evidence of the controlling role of the law in the eternal struggle for power. Although we are used to attributing the principle of the separation of powers in the state to Montesquieu's *Spirit of Laws*, just one glance at the constitutional law of the ancient Roman republic shows that the same objectives were pursued then. In ancient Rome, one did not rely on the separation of the legislature, the judiciary, and the executive; however, all public offices were based on (a) the principle of collegiality, (b) annuality, and (c) the right of intercession. That means (a) at least one fellow colleague was always appointed to work along-side an official; (b) the term of office was always for a limited period of time, usually for about a year; (c) colleagues, superiors, and tribunes of the people could exercise their veto against any measure and thus block it. The latter two restrictions, at least, are among the cornerstones of German democracy: the courts' right to intercede, and the limitation of power to the period of the electoral term of office.

Another, contemporary, example is the attempt to control the power of the banks—power that showed its most dangerous side as it threatened entire national economies during the latest financial crisis and in particular the collapse of Lehman Brothers in 2008. This event prompted the legislature of numerous states (with the involvement of the EU authorities in Brussels) to initiate a whole flood of legislative acts, which all boil down to increased control in one way or another. But even independent of actual events, in a modern state based on the rule of law, all competence standards—whether contained in the constitution, in police legislation, or in any legal act—are an attempt to control.

In addition one could also point to what is usually summarized under the concept of "laws of the market." By this one usually understands not legal statutes but economic laws. Here, too, we can actually find attempts at the creation and control of power. While an expression such as "competition is the lifeblood of business" might claim validity, it does not prevent the aspiration to and achievement of monopoly positions in the same economy. In this case legal controls in the shape of an act against restraints of competition are required in order to help the laws of the market achieve lasting success. We find similar correlations, for example, in reference to the basic principle, which says that competition is the driving force of the economy. On this basis it is, for example, only too tempting to help oneself to the trademarks of more successful competitors, in order to win greater turnover for one's own products under another label. Here, too, it is only legal statues once again—namely protection against unfair competition—that must create the framework within which the laws of the market can exercise their full effectiveness.

These few examples bear witness to the particular significance the law possesses, especially in this context.

C. SUMMARY

Beginning with the antithesis of power and powerlessness, in which the allocation of roles is by no means clear as the powerful can be powerless and vice versa, we can see that the exercise of power triggers counter-movements that try to control power. According to which power base is in question, whether it can be changed or not, the methods for controlling power are various. However, they always have the inherent characteristic that, like water in communicating vessels, they are mutually dependent.

Notes

1. Max Weber, *Economy and Society: An Outline of Interpretive Sociology*, edited by Guenther Roth and Claus Wittich (Berkeley: UCal Press, 1978), p. 531.

2. Brendan Simms, *Europe: The Struggle for Supremacy, 1453 to the Present* (London: Allen Lane, 2013).

3. Cf. Marvin Harris, *Our Kind: Who We Are, Where We Came From, Where We Are Going* (New York: Harper & Row, 1989), pp. 381 ff.

4. Victor Hugo, *The History of a Crime: the Testimony of an Eye-Witness*, trans. T.H. Joyce and Arthur Locker (New York: Mondial, 2005), p. 409. Hugo's actual words translate as: "An invasion of armies can be resisted; an invasion of ideas cannot be resisted."

5. For example as described in Heinrich Harrer, *Seven Years in Tibet: My Life Before, During and After*, trans. Richard Graves (New York: E.P. Dutton, 1954).

6. The title of the classic representative of this genre of literature, the late work by Gotthold Ephraim Lessing.

CHAPTER 11

THE POWER OF THE POWERLESS: THOUGHTS AFTER VÁCLAV HAVEL

ROGER SCRUTON

Many people in modern societies feel themselves to be entirely powerless. They contemplate in bewilderment the huge and unpredictable forces that surround them; they feel their small world constantly invaded and rearranged as a result of decisions taken by people whom they do not know and cannot influence; they watch as huge and unimaginable fortunes are suddenly bestowed on people who have done nothing to earn them, while others end a lifetime of honest labor with nothing to show for it apart from a worn-out body and a troubled soul.

Now it is fair to say that this sense of powerlessness is, in our western societies, an illusion. People have as much power as they need in order to pursue their lives according to their wishes. The law grants to all people the right to go about their business undisturbed, to own property, to engage in free transactions, to love whom they will, and to produce children of their own. The freedoms that we enjoy are sufficient, properly used, to lead a fulfilled life, according to plans of our own. If it doesn't feel like that, it is because we fail to see that control over our own private lives is all the power that we need. We fail to see that the greatest achievement of politics, and the result that guarantees all the other forms of power that are needed to pursue it, is the sovereignty of the individual.

How we use that sovereignty is up to us. Some will squander it, some will hoard it, some will use it wisely in order to express their will and to pursue their own fulfillment. We feel powerless when we contrast this great gift of sovereignty with something else that has little or nothing to do with it—the ability to purchase privileges, to accumulate resources, and to proceed through life as though never obliged to court the consent of others to what one is and does. But that feeling of powerlessness is an illusion born of resentment. The truly free person does not feel it, since resentment has been banished from his mind. The truly free person is the one who feels pleasure in the good fortune of others, and who does not envy them because he does not want what they have.

In a world where the sovereignty of the individual is guaranteed, even the wealthy and the privileged owe their power, directly or indirectly, to the consent of others. They, too, must live by agreement and not by force and, even if it is easier for them to purchase that agreement, consent matters as much to them as it does to the rest of us. This fact lies, it seems to me, at the very foundation of western democracy. Because we each enjoy sovereignty over our own lives we can give or withhold our consent in all the normal trans-actions of our daily lives. How to confer and maintain that sovereignty is, or ought to be, the major question of political philosophy in our time. It is to this goal that the discussion of human rights must be directed. How do we define those rights and how do we protect them? And of course there are vast disagreements here.

Discussion of this issue always turns me back to the great essay by Václav Havel, titled "The Power of the Powerless," written in the wake of Charter 77, the document that confronted the Communist Party of Czechoslovakia with the fact of its illegitimacy. People do not now show much understanding of what communism meant to the people of Eastern and Central Europe, and in particular they do not see that it was not a straightforward tyranny kept in place by force. It was a self-perpetuating system that survived by creating its own kind of equilibrium among those who were subject to it. People cooperated in their own enslavement, enjoying sparse but real material comforts in exchange for submission to a mechanical and impersonal power.

In such a system "they" are in charge, not "we." But we don't really know who "they" are. As in Kafka's allegory of *The Castle*, if you trace power to its source you find another powerless person. The instructions come from on high, but those on high are obeying instructions. There is a closed circle of obedience in which all are receiving orders but nobody is giving them. And nobody can say this, or even perceive it, without exposing himself to the greatest risk. Even in such a system there is a kind of social contract at work: surrender your sovereignty, the system says, and I will guarantee your security. Assert it, and you enter the unknown, where only punishment is certain.

What makes this possible? Havel makes various suggestions, but the most interesting one is this: in the post-totalitarian world, as he calls it, people learn to "live within the lie." Truth loses its central place in the affairs of government, and is replaced by ideology. By "ideology" he means a set of doctrines, slogans, epithets, and exhortations which arose from a long-refuted theory, but which remain in place, keeping vigil over human discourse, like corpses which stand to attention before every exit, snarling mechanically at anyone who tries to pass.

I first came to communist Czechoslovakia in 1979, at a time of great tension all across Eastern Europe. I did not understand very much about how people lived under communism. But the *feeling* of communism came to me immediately like a slap in the face. Without knowing the exact cause I found myself surrounded and invaded by fear. I saw faces that did not smile except sarcastically, that did not look at you except suspiciously, that did not speak except in whispers. And in everything I felt the touch of a mysterious aggression. It was as though the whole country was under threat from a secret enemy, and no one knew whence the first blow would come. It was this experience that helped me to see exactly what Havel meant when he referred to the powerless, since I had suddenly become one of them.

One of the most striking manifestations of the power by which I found myself surrounded was the proliferation on every building and in every public space of ideological slogans. Unlike the Czechs and Slovaks, who were used to these great signs—declaring the commitment to the socialist future, the fight for peace, the fraternal relations with the Soviet people, the big "No" to capitalist oppression—I could not take my eyes away from such barefaced lies, not least because they corresponded to the lies taught to students in our own Marxist university departments. As Havel memorably wrote, the customers of the greengrocer who places the sign bearing the words "Workers of the world unite!" in his window notice only that today there are carrots, but no tomatoes. Like the greengrocer they treat the official words as irrelevant, ritual formulae which are repeated because required, like the "amen" at the end of a prayer, and which have no significance in themselves.

Perhaps the most important thing that I learned on my subsequent visits was that ideology is not thought but its opposite—the thing that makes thinking impossible, by blocking up the channels through which truth can enter the mind. As Havel put the point:

> The post-totalitarian system touches people at
> every step, but it does so with its ideological gloves
> on. This is why life in the system is so thoroughly
> permeated with hypocrisy and lies: government
> by bureaucracy is called popular government; the

working class is enslaved in the name of the working class; the complete degradation of the individual is presented as his ultimate liberation; depriving people of information is called making it available; the use of power to manipulate is called the public control of power, and the arbitrary abuse of power is called observing the legal code; the repression of culture is called its development; the expansion of imperial influence is presented as support for the oppressed; the lack of free expression becomes the highest form of freedom; farcical elections become the highest form of democracy; banning independent thought becomes the most scientific of world views; military occupation becomes fraternal assistance. Because the regime is captive to its own lies, it must falsify everything. It falsifies the past. It falsifies the present, and it falsifies the future. It falsifies statistics. It pretends not to possess an omnipotent and unprincipled police apparatus. It pretends to respect human rights. It pretends to persecute no one. It pretends to fear nothing. It pretends to pretend nothing.

I had travelled in order to address a private seminar in Prague, and as a result I fell in with a group of young people who, for a variety of reasons, had been excluded from the educational system, and who were hungry for the information that I had brought to them from afar. I quickly came to see that they were not in any real sense "dissidents." They were not people who had shaped their lives as "opponents of the system," or followers of some rival ideology. Like Havel, I learned to put the word "dissident" in inverted commas. For the people I met were simply those who had retreated to another place beneath the city, a strange and quiet catacomb, where they tried to live in truth. Living in truth brought fatigue and privations, and never has its atmosphere been so effectively caught as by Havel, in his play *Largo Desolato*, written in 1984, and first appearing in samizdat after my visits came to an end, following my arrest and expulsion.

Havel had seen, with characteristic insight, that where the ruling power has no authority, the search for authority—even if it is only a charismatic and personal authority—brings power of another kind, power that is effective in ways that the "authorities," as they ironically called themselves, could not hope to enjoy. This was the power to move people's hearts and souls, and to join with them in what Jan Patočka called "the solidarity of the shattered." It was a power that came from placing truth where it belongs, at the center of your life, and at the beginning and end of your discourse. Havel captured the idea in memorable words:

> The crust presented by the life of lies is made of strange stuff. As long as it seals off hermetically the entire society, it appears to be made of stone. But the moment someone breaks through in one place, when

one person cries out, "The emperor is naked!"—when
a single person breaks the rules of the game, thus
exposing it as a game—everything suddenly appears
in another light and the whole crust seems then to be
made of a tissue on the point of tearing and disinte-
grating uncontrollably.

Havel had burst through that crust and had been immediately seized and punished for doing so. A great effort
had been made to repair the crust, so that the illusion
could be restored that it was made of stone. But beneath
the crust, in a system of catacombs dug out over years,
young people were experimenting with the thing that
the system denied, which was sovereignty. They were
making choices for their lives, and endeavoring to "live
in truth." To be part of that endeavor was, for me, a
transforming experience. Over the years, working
together with western colleagues, I joined the underground university in Prague and Brno, which was
not so much a university as a network of sympathy in
which art, music, philosophy, history, and literature
were wrapped together in classes designed to teach the
habit of distinguishing the true from the false. I was
not optimistic that it would lead to anything: unlike
Havel, I was convinced that the crust above my head
was made of stone. But it was a moving and instructive
experience to find myself among people for whom the

most important question to be asked of anything you said was whether it was true, and if so what followed. I came to understand then the extent to which the ideological disease had penetrated western universities also, and the extent to which living in truth is a challenge in every place where career and comfort conflict with it.

Well, you might say, all that may be interesting enough, but it belongs to the past, to a bleak period of European history from which we have moved on. It is no longer relevant to our problems today. However, that is not the conclusion that I draw, and I will conclude this essay by saying why. In placing truth at the center of their lives, my friends and students of those days were also affirming their sovereignty against the system. Although the sphere of their choice was narrow, and the light in the catacombs pale and vacillating, they had recognized the deep connection between truth and freedom. To live in truth means to take responsibility for what you think and say. You become answerable for your words, your beliefs, your vision of the world, and this is the very opposite of the life required by ideology. Everywhere you confront the question, posed by others and by the life around you, whether what you think or say is true. This question is hard. You don't answer it by avoiding it, and if you answer it sincerely you must also live by what you say.

But if you are responsible for your beliefs, how much more are you responsible for your actions, for your feelings, for your posture towards others and the world? This was what was taught by the "life in truth"— namely responsibility, *Verantwortung*. You are not free just because you can do what you want, or satisfy your appetites. The post-totalitarian system was constructed by organizing people's appetites so that they could easily obey them. They did what they wanted: but did it without consulting others, without evaluating their own actions, without taking responsibility for their shared *Lebenswelt*. True sovereignty, true freedom, true responsibility are one and the same—a posture towards the world that it is natural for us to acquire, but which can also be easily destroyed by fear and manipulation.

The people whom I knew in the catacombs were keeping alive the habits that make it possible to take responsibility for the way things are. It is, in my view, no accident that the first two prime ministers of the Czech and Slovak lands were graduates of our underground university, or that so many subsequently prominent figures were educated there. For all the troubles and uncertainties that followed the collapse of the Berlin Wall, it has been understood that the new society depends upon the consent of its members, that you can build consent only through the sovereignty of the individual, and that sovereignty means responsibility.

And here I would venture to draw a contrast with the so-called Arab Spring. In the days of Muammar Gaddafi in Libya people were powerless, as they were under communism. But they were also oppressed. They were not asked to cooperate in their enslavement: they were simply given no choice in the matter. And there were no catacombs, no networks or structures that kept alive the memory of another way of being. The default position for Libyans, then as now, was the retreat into "the shade of the Koran," as Sayyid Qutb described it—to give up on politics, on freedom, and on sovereignty, and to submit to a document that purports to be the word of God and which promises rewards in another world than this one. In such circumstances you can remove the tyrant, and people will cooperate in helping you. There will be a moment of rejoicing. But no one will come forward with plans for a new kind of government, in which the sovereignty of the individual would be put at the top of the agenda. The only person to come forward is the next tyrant, or the gang of ardent young men who are looking for him.

Of course there are many factors at work in the chaos of the Middle East other than the lack of the underground networks of powerless people. Nevertheless, in the circumstances that prevailed in that region prior to the Arab Spring, the powerless did not exercise their power. There was not, as there was in Eastern and Central Europe, the memory of another kind of power than the one under which people suffered. The only idea for a better future was to *replace the powerful*, not to *advance the powerless*. The kind of power of which Havel wrote is precisely not exercised through coercion, dominion, or violence. It is the power that resides in truth itself, in the ability to stand before the other in open dialogue, and to recognize that he has the right to disagree.

What is it about our history and our social institutions that makes it so easy for us to see that there is power of that kind, and that the powerless too can enjoy it? Let me venture a suggestion. We Europeans are products of a religion and a political tradition that have put the sovereign individual at the heart of the moral order. We accept the need for government, but only if it is *limited* government, which leaves the sphere of individual choice intact. We see the role of government in the religious life as that of guaranteeing religious freedom, rather than imposing

213

religious conformity. And while we accept the right of governments to tax us and to regulate our economic life, we are jealous of our free agreements, and resist the attempts by governments to undo or control them. All this comes from a long tradition of taking responsibility for our lives, of confessing to our faults and trying to rectify them, of accepting that the truth is more important than the fictions that make it easy to be governed. And the great question in my mind is whether that long tradition is coming to an end. Many people warn us, now, against the increasing level of censorship in our societies, against the intrusive presence of the managerial state in all our decisions, against the ways in which associations are controlled and opinions anathematized in the name of emerging secular orthodoxies. And if these warnings are in any way justified, perhaps we need again to take a lesson from Havel, and recognize that the powerless too have power in the face of them. Maybe the time has come once again to dig those catacombs, and to build in them the shrines to our civilization that will keep the memory of it alive.

CONTRIBUTORS

Simon Denny was born in Auckland, New Zealand, in 1982. He holds a BFA from Auckland University (2004) and an MFA (2009) from the Frankfurt Städelschule, and has taken part in four residencies split between Western Europe and Australia (2007–12). He uses tech-centric sculptures to convey his critical and creative responses to the contested space of the media-sphere. He attracted international attention and received outstanding criticism for his works *New Management* (2014), Portikus, Frankfurt, *The Innovator's Dilemma* (2015), MoMA, PS1, New York, and his show *Secret Power* (2015) in the New Zealand Pavilion at the 56th Venice Biennale. Simon Denny observes the entertainment industry's various media, its aesthetics, and the inflationary information economy underlying it. He uses its images and objects for his sculptures and installations. Further solo exhibitions held at the Aspen Art Museum, Aspen, at Westfälischer Kunstverein, Münster, at Petzel Gallery, New York, and at Neuer Aachener Kunstverein, Aachen, among other locations. Between November 2015 and February 2016, he exhibited his work *Products for Organising* at the Serpentine Gallery, London.

Dr. Corinne Michaela Flick studied both law and literature, taking American studies as her subsidiary. She gained her Dr. phil. in 1989. She has worked as in-house lawyer for Bertelsmann Buch AG and Amazon.com. In 1998 she became General Partner in Vivil GmbH und Co. KG, Offenburg. She is Founder and Chair of the Convoco Foundation.

Dr. Flick is Chair of the Board of Trustees of the Aspen Institute, Germany; member of the board of the Alfred Herrhausen Society, the international forum of Deutsche Bank; member of the board of the Osterfestspiele Salzburg; and a member of the Executive Committee of the International Council of the Tate Gallery, London.

Prof. Dr. Clemens Fuest gained his doctorate at the University of Cologne in 1994 and his postdoctoral qualification at the Ludwig Maximilian University of Munich in 2000. From 2001 he was Professor of Political Economy at the University of Cologne, from 2004 Visiting Professor at Bocconi University in Milan, and 2008–13 Professor of Business Taxation and Research Director of the Oxford University Centre for Business Taxation. Between 2013 and 2015, he was President and Director of Science and Research of the Centre for European Economic Research (ZEW) and Professor of Economics at the University of Mannheim.

Since 2016 he has been President of the ifo Institute for Economic Research in Munich. Clemens Fuest has been a member of the Academic Advisory Board of the German Federal Ministry of Finance since 2003 and Head of the Board 2007–10. In October 2012 he became a member of the Advisory Board for Sustainable Development of the State Government of Baden-Württemberg. He has been a member of The Market Economy Foundation's scientific council *Kronberger Kreis* 2004–8, and again as of March 2013. Since 2014 he has been a member of the EU High-Level Group on Own Resources, and since 2015 a member of the German Minimum Wage Commission. He is Programme Director of the Oxford University Centre for Business Taxation, a member of numerous German and international scientific academies and associations, and is on the board of the International Institute for Public Finance. He is editor of *Beiträge zur Finanzwissenschaft* [Contributions to Financial Research] and on several editorial boards of scientific journals.

Prof. Dr. Thomas Hoeren studied theology and law at the Universities of Tübingen, Münster, and London 1980–87. In 1989 he gained his doctorate, and in 1994 his postdoctoral qualification from Münster University. In 1995–7 he was Professor at the Faculty of Law of the Heinrich-Heine-University, Düsseldorf. In 1996–2012 he was a part-time judge at the Düsseldorf Appeal Court. Since April 1997 he has been Professor of Information, Media and Business Law at the University of Münster and Head of the Institute for Information, Telecommunication and Media Law (ITM). He is Adjunct Professor at the Fraunhofer Institute for Applied Information Technology (FIT). He is a domain-name arbitrator for the World Intellectual Property Organization (WIPO) and the European Commission. In 2012–14 he was Dean of the Faculty of Law at Münster University. His professional appointments and memberships include: Research Fellow at the Oxford Internet Institute, Balliol College, in 2004; Lecturer in Information and IT Law at the Universities of Zurich and Vienna;

Member of the Expert Committee for Copyright and Publishing Law at the German Union for Intellectual Property Protection; since 2006 personal tutor at the Studienstiftung des Deutschen Volkes; in 2005 he received the Alcatel-SEL Foundation research prize for "technical communication." Since April 2015 he has been a spokesman for the Federal Ministry of Education and Research's major research project ABIDA (Assessing Big Data).

Ambassador Wolfgang Ischinger is Chairman of the Munich Security Conference as well as member of the council of the German Institute for International and Security Affairs. He is on the Governing Board of the Stockholm International Peace Research Institute, the American Academy Berlin, the Hertie School of Governance, and other non-profit institutions.

After studying law and political sciences in Bonn, Geneva, and Harvard he joined the German Foreign Office in 1975. In 1998–2001 he was Deputy Foreign Minister in the Foreign Office; in 2001–6 German Ambassador to the USA; in 2006–8 German Ambassador in London. In 1995–98 he led the German delegation in Dayton, Ohio during the Bosnia peace talks in the Kosovo crisis, and in negotiations concerning the NATO-Russia Founding Act.

In 2007 he was the EU Representative in the Troika negotiations on the status of Kosovo. In 2012 he was appointed by President Hollande to the commission drafting the French White Paper on Defense and National Security, and in spring 2014 he represented the OSCE in efforts to create a national dialogue in Ukraine. Since December 2014 he has chaired the OSCE panel of "Eminent Persons."

He is Honorary Professor at the University of Tübingen, and in 2015 became Senior Professor at the Hertie School of Governance. He has been awarded the Order of Merit of the Federal Republic of Germany, alongside numerous foreign orders and distinctions.

Prof. Dr. Stefan Korioth gained his doctorate in law in 1990 and completed his postdoctoral qualification in public and constitutional law. From 1996 to 2000 he was Professor of Public Law, Constitutional History, and Theory of Government at Greifswald. In 2000 he accepted the Chair of Public and Ecclesiastical Law at LMU, Munich. His publications include *Integration und Bundesstaat* (1990), *Der Finanzausgleich zwischen Bund und Ländern* (1997), *Grundzüge des Staatskirchenrechts* (with B. Jean d'Heur, 2000), and *Das Bundesverfassungsgericht* (with Klaus Schlaich, 9th edition, 2012).

Hans Ulrich Obrist is Co-director of the Serpentine Galleries, London. Prior to this, he was curator of the Musée d'Art Moderne de la Ville, Paris. Since his first show World Soup (The Kitchen Show) in 1991 he has curated more than 250 exhibitions. In 2009 Obrist was made Honorary Fellow of the Royal Institute of British Architects (RIBA), and in 2011 received the CCS Bard Award for Curatorial Excellence. Obrist has lectured internationally at academic and art institutions, and is contributing editor to several magazines and journals. Obrist's recent publications include *A Brief History of Curating, Everything You Always Wante* to Know About Curating But Were Afrai* to Ask, Do It: The Compen*ium, Think Like Clou*s, Ai Weiwei Speaks, Ways of Curating,* and new volumes of his *Conversation Series.*

Prof. Dr. Christoph G. Paulus studied law at Munich, taking his doctorate in law in 1980. His postdoctoral qualification, gained in 1991, was in civil law, civil procedure, and Roman law, for which he was awarded the Medal of the University of Paris II. He received his LL.M. at Berkeley in 1983/1984 and returned to Berkeley between 1989 and 1990 as a recipient of a Feodor Lynen Stipend from the Humboldt Foundation. In 1992–94 he was Associate Professor at Augsburg, and from the summer semester 1994 he was at the

Law Faculty of the Humboldt University in Berlin, becoming Dean of the Faculty in 2008–10. In 2009 he was made Director of the Research Center Institute for Interdisciplinary Restructuring, and Consultant to the International Monetary Fund and the World Bank. Among other roles he is member (and Director) of the International Insolvency Institute of the American College of Bankruptcy and the International Association for Procedural Law. Since 2006 he has been advisor on insolvency law to the German delegation to UNCITRAL. He is on the editorial board of the *Zeitschrift für Wirtschaftsrecht* (ZIP), the *Norton Annual Review of International Insolvency*, and the *International Insolvency Law Review*, among other journals.

Prof. Dr. Albrecht Ritschl has been Professor of Economic History at the London School of Economics since 2007. He was previously Professor of Economics at Humboldt University of Berlin, at the University of Zurich, as well as Associate Professor of Economics at Pompeu Fabra University from 1994 to 1999. He has held visiting fellowships at Princeton University and at the University of Pennsylvania. He is a Fellow at the Centre for Economic Policy Research (CEPR), the Centre for Economic Performance (CEP), as well as at CESifo. He is a member of the Scientific Advisory

Board to the German Ministry of Economics. He holds both a doctoral and postdoctoral qualification from the University of Munich. He has published extensively on German economic history in the 20th century, with a focus on the Great Depression and the 1930s. He received wide press coverage for his warnings against an overly strict approach towards the Greek debt problem. Currently he is spokesman for an expert commission researching the history of the German Ministry of Economics and its predecessors since 1919.

Prof. Jörg Rocholl, Ph.D. is President of ESMT European School of Management and Technology in Berlin and holds the Ernst & Young Chair in Governance and Compliance. He graduated from the Universität Witten/Herdecke, where he earned a degree in economics (with honors). After completing his Ph.D. at Columbia University in New York, he was named an Assistant Professor at the University of North Carolina at Chapel Hill. He has researched and taught at ESMT since 2007 and was appointed President of ESMT in 2011. He is a member of the Economic Advisory Board of the German Federal Ministry of Finance, Research Professor at the ifo Institute in Munich, and Duisenberg Fellow of the European Central Bank (ECB).

Professor Brendan Simms, Ph.D. studied at Trinity College, Dublin, the University of Tübingen, and gained his doctorate at Peterhouse, Cambridge, in 1993, where he has since been a Fellow. Before that he was a Research Fellow at Christ Church, Oxford, 1992–93. From 1998–2008 he was first a Lecturer, then a Reader at the Centre of International Studies, Cambridge. Since 2008 he has been Professor of the History of European International Relations in the Department of Politics and International Studies, Cambridge. He has been Director of the Centre of International Studies since 2009. He is a member of the Academic Advisory Council of the Leibniz Institute for European History, Mainz. He is recipient of among other prizes the Thirlwall Prize and Seeley Medal of the University of Cambridge. He is currently establishing the Centre of Geopolitics and Grand Strategy at Cambridge, a new interdisciplinary center for the study of grand strategy and statecraft, as well as the think tank Project for Democratic Union which promotes a full political union of the Eurozone on Anglo-American lines.

Prof. Roger Scruton, Ph.D. is currently a Senior Research Fellow of Blackfriars Hall, Oxford, and Senior Fellow at the Ethics and Public Policy Center,

Washington, DC. He was for a while employed by Birkbeck College in the University of London, but since 1990 has been self-employed. He is author of over 40 books, including works of criticism, political theory, and aesthetics, as well as novels and short stories. His writings include *The Aesthetics of Music* (1997), *Death-Devotel Heart: Sex anl the Sacrel in Wagner's Tristan anl Isolle* (2003), *Unlerstanling Music* (2009), *The Face of Gol* (2011), *The Soul of the Worll* (2014), and *Notes from Unlergrounl* (2014). Roger Scruton is a Fellow of the Royal Society of Literature, a Fellow of the European Academy of Arts and Sciences, and a Fellow of the British Academy.

TO DO OR NOT TO DO—INACTION AS A FORM OF
ACTION
2015

ISBN: 978-0-9931953-0-3

*With contributions by: Bazon Brock, Gert-Rudolf Flick,
Peter M. Huber, Kai A. Konrad, Stefan Korioth, Friedhelm
Mennekes, Hans Ulrich Obrist and Marina Abramović,
Christoph G. Paulus, Jörg Rocholl, Wolfgang Schön, Roger
Scruton, Pirmin Stekeler-Weithofer*

DEALING WITH DOWNTURNS: STRATEGIES IN
UNCERTAIN TIMES
2014

ISBN: 978-0-9572958-8-9

*With contributions by: Jens Beckert, Bazon Brock, Saul
David, Gerd Gigerenzer, Paul Kirchhof, Kai A. Konrad,
Stefan Korioth, Christoph G. Paulus, Jörg Rocholl, Burkhard
Schwenker*

COLLECTIVE LAW-BREAKING—A THREAT TO
LIBERTY
2013

ISBN: 978-0-9572958-5-8

*With contributions by: Shaukat Aziz, Roland Berger,
Christoph G. Paulus, Ingolf Pernice, Wolfgang Schön,
Hannes Siegrist, Jürgen Stark, Pirmin Stekeler-Weithofer*

WHO OWNS THE WORLD'S KNOWLEDGE?
2012

ISBN: 978-0-9572958-0-3

*With contributions by: Eckhard Cordes, Urs Gasser, Thomas
Hoeren, Viktor Mayer-Schönberger, Christoph G. Paulus,
Jürgen Renn, Burkhard Schwenker and Hannes Siegrist*

CAN'T PAY, WON'T PAY? SOVEREIGN DEBT AND
THE CHALLENGE OF GROWTH IN EUROPE
2011

ISBN: 978-0-9572958-3-4

*With contributions by: Roland Berger, Howard Davies,
Otmar Issing, Paul Kirchhof, Kai A. Konrad, Stefan Korioth,
Christoph G. Paulus and Burkhard Schwenker*

www.ingramcontent.com/pod-product-compliance
Lightning Source LLC
Chambersburg PA
CBHW060035030426

42334CB00019B/2342